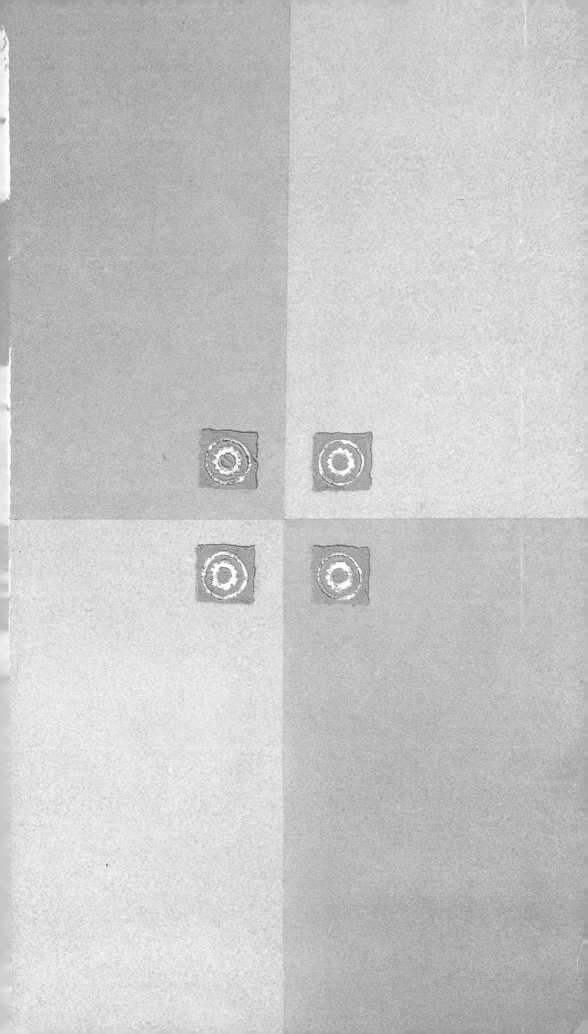

DECORATIVE

Paint

RECIPES

A STEP-BY-STEP GUIDE
TO FINISHING TOUCHES
FOR YOUR HOME

**Richard Lowther and
Lynne Robinson**

CHRONICLE BOOKS
SAN FRANCISCO

Front cover: *Checkerboard table tops (pages 172–5)*
Back cover: *Stamped squiggles on stripes (pages 92–5)*
p. 1: *Stippled wall with embossed motif (pages 110–13)*
pp. 2–3: *A floor covered in giant painted daisies (pages 116–19)*
p. 4: *A wall stamped with striped checks (pages 88–91)*
p. 5: *Stenciled fruits decorate a bar front (pages 100–103)*

Warning

Always make certain that your workplace is safe and your tools and materials are in the proper condition. You should be sure to follow the manufacturer's operating instructions, obey all local laws and codes, take safety precautions, and use your best judgment. All do-it-yourself projects involve some risk, and the publisher takes no responsibility for any injury or loss arising from the procedures or materials described in this book. Materials, tools, skills , and work areas vary greatly and are the responsibility of the reader.

First published in the United States in 1997 by Chronicle Books

Interior design and layout by Quadrille Publishing Limited
Cover design by Karen Smidth
Cover photography by Debbie Patterson (projects), Nicki Dowey (swatches)

Library of Congress Cataloging-in-Publication Data available

ISBN 0-8118-1848-9

Printed and bound in Spain

Distributed in Canada by Raincoast Books
8680 Cambie Street
Vancouver, B.C. V6P 6M9

10 9 8 7 6 5 4 3 2 1

Chronicle Books
85 Second Street
San Francisco, CA 94105

Web Site: www.chronbooks.com

CONTENTS

INTRODUCTION

This book is for people who would like to get more involved with, and have control over, decorating the interior of their homes with paint. We hope it will provide a way forward for those who want to do more than just buy the current color at the local paint store and roller it on the wall, yet are afraid of the color chaos that might result if they are let loose without any guidance.

We set out to show how color, texture, and pattern can come together in designs which have a certain vitality, whether it be radiated out in highly charged contrasts or in a quiet and stylish manner. At its heart are over one hundred and twenty paint recipes that, like those in a cookbook, can either be followed teaspoon for teaspoon, or can be used as a point of departure for you to develop and realize your own ideas. Although we make use of one or two paint effects and the occasional false finish, this is not a book full of arcane recipes with hard-to-find ingredients that require beautiful and maybe strange brushes for their application. In other words, it is not a book for people who like alchemy. In fact, the tools we use most of the time are somewhat ordinary brushes, household sponges, and paint rollers, while our standard paint is nothing more exotic than plain, ordinary latex.

However, although we have chosen the equipment and materials to be as simple as possible, there will always remain, for those who want to abandon plain white interiors, the difficult question of which colors to choose. Decisions about color are always going to give pause for reflection. There was a time when rules of taste gave guidance, but late twentieth-century culture has managed to reject almost all of these. Blue with green can now be seen. You may choose colors because of the memories they evoke, for cultural reasons, because they are soothing. These choices are all personal, and only you can make them. You may seek guidance in color theory, but understanding the spectrum and how to mix paint will not be much

Left: Our own seedheads have the look of a handpainted design but are in fact part of a stenciled frieze worked using colorwashes and spray-wax resist. Torn paper masks off areas that are not being painted.

Left: At Charleston, their home in Sussex, England, the artists Vanessa Bell and Duncan Grant painted these softly colored random stripes across a wall. The blue doors merge with the design while real objects blend happily with *trompe l'oeil.*

help in choosing which colors to use, although it can explain why certain color combinations behave the way they do. I know of only one artist who derives inspiration from the color wheel. The rest spend more time looking at other painters' work. We believe a lot can be learned by looking, and this partly explains why there is such a broad range of color combinations given in this book. We usually show two or three alternative color combinations for each design. This not only gives you a choice, but we hope it will let you see the effect a change of color, be it ever so small, can have. You also have the option to use a recipe from elsewhere in the book if it is more in keeping with your scheme. But whatever you do, you should always look at other interiors, at textiles, clothing, and painting, and take your lead from those you like.

Above: A staircase is an excellent place to introduce decorative motifs. Whimsical spirals have been applied beneath a fantasy painted molding.

The colors we wear are influenced by fashion. So too with interiors, except we often have to live in buildings which were built many decades ago. Do not let this trouble you. With care we can combine the old with the new. You can have respect for the old, even venerate it, but that does not mean you have to live in a timewarp. Nevertheless, we personally have been influenced by a lot of what we have seen from the past, not least because the colors of old, derived from natural pigments, have a quality we happen to like.

INTRODUCTION

In addition to choosing and mixing colors, you will have to arrange them into shapes on your surface. We realize that many of you will lack the confidence to develop a pattern or draw a motif. In the realm of pattern, fashion again exerts its influence. The mood is a lot more individual than it was twenty years ago, softer but full of vitality. The *fleur de lis* of old has been replaced by the altogether more lively spiral. Some design classics will always remain, but they can adapt to suit the current mood or look. One example of this is stripes. These seem to change their personality each season. One year all slim and Regency, they reappear the next as broad and Gustavian. Whatever form they take, you know that stripes will bring a great sense of style to a room.

While stripes seem to go naturally on a wall, checks gravitate all too readily onto the floor. This is not a hard and fast rule though, so try applying your checks to walls, window frames, or even furniture.

Applying checks and stripes needs only the skill of planning and layout, and maybe some dexterous use of masking tape. Other designs can be helped onto walls or floors with stencils and stamps. These are an excellent way of controlling where your paint goes, as well as a means of covering a surface quickly. In most cases, at the back of this book, we give the motifs for the stencils and stamps we use. You can trace and enlarge them to the size you require, then transfer them to your surface. You will see that our designs tend toward the simple. Over- complicated motifs can look dated and fussy.

Our first choice of paint is flat vinyl latex. We buy it in white and in basic colors like red and black. We then change it by adding pigments, usually in the form of artists' acrylic colors. Good-quality water-based colors have all the qualities we ask for in a paint for home decoration. Not only do they give an excellent finish, but they dry quickly, do not smell too bad, clean easily, and they do not cause as much damage to the environment as oil-based paint. And perhaps most important, since

Above: A door decorated with handpainted motifs which could equally well have been carried out with stenciling or stamping techniques. Note, too, the simple painted border.

we see our interiors as nonstatic and ever in need of revision, latex paint can be painted over without much fuss. We occasionally use oil-based paints because they can be harder-wearing, but we find that modern acrylic paints and varnishes are usually tough enough for the average home.

The selection of artists' acrylic colors far exceeds what we need to color our latex. These modern liquid pigments are completely safe to handle. This could not be said about some of their forebears. They may have had curious or romantic names such as dragon's blood, bladder green, or caput mortuum, but many were lethal. It is said that Napoleon died from inhaling the arsenic fumes coming off the emerald-green pigment in his wallpaper. Having interiors to die for is of course just an expression these days. Still, do be very careful.

Above: Forming a frame above the fireplace and running along the baseboard, this simple design could be painted using the edge of a sponge dipped in red paint.

Right: Notre-Dame-la-Grande, Poitiers, like so many Romanesque churches in France, is decorated with geometric patterns rarely repeated from pillar to pillar, a wonderful source of inspiration for those who like strong patterns and natural earth coloring.

PART ONE

A GOOD FOUNDATION

A look at the practical side of decorating with a guide to tools, equipment, and materials, mixing colors, preparation, and planning, as well as making and using stamps, stencils, and masks.

A checkerboard table top (see pages 172–5) in vivid sage green and red relies on a steady hand to paint the checks on top of the sponged-on base coat. Artists' brushes, screw-top jars for mixing the paint, and some saucers to use as palettes are the only equipment you will need for this stage.

If, as we suggest, you are to sidestep the impositions of the paint manufacturers and blend your own colors, you need to be able to predict what might happen. It is encouraging to know that color can only be changed in three ways.

Wishing something paler is wanting a change of *tone*, and is most commonly achieved by the addition of white. To go darker, we may add black, but often raw umber is a better choice, giving softer, more natural tones. To reduce a color's brightness means changing its *intensity* or *chroma* without changing its tone. Adding gray will achieve this; but match the gray to the color—a dark one for dark colors and a pale one for light colors. To change red to orange—in other words to change the red's *hue*—add yellow. Attempting to change to a particular hue may not be possible, though. For example, changing red to purple by adding blue is particularly problematic.

When choosing colors to use in combination, it is useful to limit yourself to a single hue and vary the tone only within the design. Or color a design with only three or four hues, all of the same grayness or intensity. Working within disciplines such as these will prevent you from creating visual pandemonium—while avoiding the trap of being too timid and painting your walls antique white.

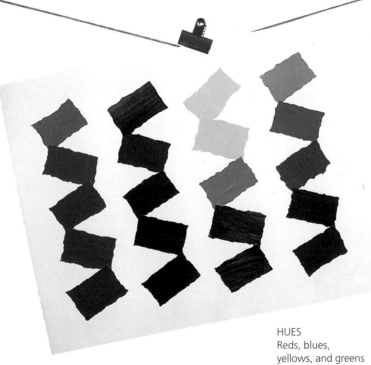

HUES
Reds, blues, yellows, and greens are all different hues. In theory you can mix two primary hues together to make oranges, greens, and purples, but in practice it is better to buy these colors if you want pure, intense pigment. This applies to the earth colors, too.

TONES

Tones or tints are achieved through the addition of white to a hue. To make a shade, you can add black, as we did to this blue, but with some colors this may also result in a change of hue. Here, besides being made paler with white, the ocher has been gradually toned down with raw umber, and the red with burnt umber.

INTENSITY

When you want to subdue a color without changing its tone, add gray. The gray may be bought ready-mixed, or mixed from black and white. Intensity will always be reduced, too, when you add other hues, especially the earth colors. Colors that contain gray or an earth color form the basis of many of our recipes.

THE PAINT

Almost all the projects in this book have been carried out with modern, water-based paints. They are easy and safe to work with, usually odorless, and quick to dry. If you prefer to use oil-based media or traditional water-based paints, such as milk paints, you will have to adjust the coloring material to suit, as indicated in the chart below. You will also have to make allowances for the differences in the way these paints behave.

At the heart of many of our recipes is white latex flat paint. Choose a high-quality one. Paints offered at bargain prices may be tempting, but in our experience they are loaded with so much chalky pigment that the resulting finish is not only lamentable, it is also much too absorbent for many of our paint techniques. High-quality latex paints perform well and make an excellent base for the addition of color. When we want a dark tone, we start with a color base close to our goal—a black or a red, for example.

To color the paint, we rely almost exclusively on artists' acrylic colors, and have used these throughout, unless otherwise stated. Although they are expensive compared to ordinary interior paint, the quality of the pigment is high and you need only a little to bring about a color change. Just occasionally we make use of powder pigments. Unfortunately, many of these are toxic, especially if inhaled or handled. If you are using these, refer carefully to the manufacturers' instructions.

You could use latex semigloss paint instead of latex flat, if you prefer a finish with a slight sheen. Its color can also be modified by the addition of artists' acrylic colors.

PAINT TYPE	COLOR WITH	THIN WITH
WATER-BASED		
• Latex flat	• Artists' acrylic color	• Water
• Latex semigloss	• Powder pigment	
• Decorators' acrylic	• Tinting color	
• Acrylic glazing liquid		
• Casein/milk paint	• Powder pigment	• Water
OIL-BASED		
• Alkyd gloss	• Artists' oil color	• Mineral spirits
• Alkyd eggshell/satin	• Powder pigment	
• Floor paint	• Tinting color	
• Oil glazing liquid		

LATEX PAINTS

Besides being widely available, latex paints readily mix with artists' acrylic colors. Four of these swatches began life as brilliant white. The fifth has black as its base. Each has had one or more colors added to produce the hues you see here.

POWDER PIGMENTS

These are a way to color paint. Their advantage is that they can be mixed with any type of paint. This can be handy if you are using a mix of media, for example latex for walls and oil-based paint for door and window frames. The color range is smaller than that of artists' acrylics—for example, you will not find neutral gray—but it does include metallic finishes, which the artists' acrylics do not.

ARTISTS' ACRYLIC COLORS

These are available in more hues than is strictly necessary. Buy top-quality products for the strongest pigments. Normally sold as a rather thick paste, which is useful for stenciling and similar applications, they are also available from some manufacturers in a more fluid consistency. The color is just as powerful, but it is easier to brush out or apply with a roller, and it mixes more readily with latex paint.

SPECIAL PAINTS

Latex paint provides a fairly tough finish and, in conjunction with varnish, can be use for a surprising number of applications. Some of our floors and table tops have latex paint as their base.

Latex can be turned into a customized paint by the addition of white glue or acrylic glazing liquid. White glue will strengthen the latex paint and can act like a glaze by thinning the paint out without making it too liquid. Acrylic glazing liquid is an expensive polyvinyl chloride or acrylic-based paint additive. It extends the drying time of the paint, and increases its translucency, so making it easier to carry out some of our decorative treatments.

Occasionally we have used a special paint to satisfy a particular need. Some of those on the market can be made at home, but one we do like is an acrylic-based paint formulated to look like milk paint. It dries to a matte finish and, if you wish, can be rubbed back to imitate the wear and patina of an old piece of painted furniture. Such treatment, popular though it is, belies one of milk paint's most notable characteristics—the fact that it is hardwearing and extremely durable.

Other special paints are sometimes needed for fitness of purpose rather than for their looks. A painted wooden or concrete floor needs to be especially well-sealed and durable. For our concrete floor on pages 120-23, we chose an oil-based floor paint. It is intended for use on garage and car showroom floors, so it should stand up to normal domestic wear and tear.

Artists' suppliers stock a wealth of other special products. Among these are glass paints, one of which is used to create stained-glass effects, while another is a frosting varnish which is an alternative to having your windows acid-etched or sandblasted. You are unlikely to fool anyone with these products, so simply treat them as decorative paints, just as we do.

MILK PAINTS
These are not always available, but they can be made at home from casein, borax, and powder pigments. The result will be a breathing, non-toxic, traditional paint. Modern versions—also non-toxic—are bound with acrylic.

FLOOR PAINTS
These come in a wide variety of media but not always in a wide range of colors. Here we show one bound with an alkyd resin—the most common binder for all kinds of modern household paints—reinforced with polyurethane for extra hardness. Choose a satin finish. A gloss finish will highlight any imperfections, which will all too easily be seen on a floor because of the angle at which daylight usually strikes it.

GLASS PAINTS

GLASS PAINTS
These are quick-drying, almost impossible to brush out smoothly, highly flammable, and cannot take a second coat as the solvent in the paint softens the paint below. If you are prepared for all that, you can achieve some colorful results with them.

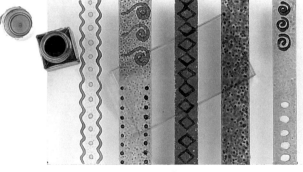

FROSTING VARNISHES
Acrylic-based, these are more user-friendly than other glass paints. They produce a convincing frosted finish when sponged on and can be tinted or, as here, colored with metallic and irides-cent powders. For an etched-glass look, use them with stencils or masking tape, but don't be afraid to brush or stamp them on, too.

MIXING PAINTS

Adding colors to one another will bring about a change of hue, tone, or intensity, and possibly all three (see page 14). Few of the color mixes we use are very intense, since most include gray or are mixed with one of the earth colors—the oxides, umbers, ochers, and siennas. These, apart from being wonderful colors in their own right, can tone and subdue colors in a far more subtle way than black or white alone.

To ensure that our color-mixing is as predictable as possible, we normally color only with artists' acrylic colors made from a single classifiable pigment. Each pigment has a reference number, and high-grade paints should give details of the pigments they contain. Thus Mars red is in fact PR101, a single pigment sometimes called red iron oxide or Venetian red. These single-pigment colors should also make using the recipes foolproof. However, in a few cases we have used a ready-mixed latex paint, which bears different names, depending on the manufacturer. Here we have used a descriptive term (such as "lemon yellow" or "pimento red") that is sufficiently familiar to most people that you should have little trouble duplicating the effect shown.

GLAZES
You can change the translucency of paint by adding water. Add too much, though, and it will become runny, and the binder will be so weakened that the paint will be wiped off the wall at the next spring-cleaning. Adding a glazing liquid to a paint overcomes this problem and also has the advantage of increasing the paint's working time. This is a great help when you want to color-wash, stipple, sponge, or dry brush.

WHITE BASE
This group of recipes all start with white latex flat paint. Some of them include grays, some earth colors, some both. The swatch on top has had yellow ocher and ultramarine added, while the next is the white with yellow ocher and Payne's gray. The third mix is with dioxazine purple and Payne's gray, the fourth with raw sienna and magenta, and the last is the white plus cadmium yellow.

GREEN BASE
These swatches show what an extremely powerful pigment phthalocyanine green is. You need only a little in any mixture, and even then the color may be too garish. On the right of this trio, the green has been subdued with raw umber, while on the left it has been darkened with Payne's gray.

YELLOW BASE
If you try to darken cadmium yellow with, say, Payne's gray, it will turn toward green as shown on the left of this trio. Instead, try one of the earth colors such as raw umber, as seen on the right.

BLUE BASE
Cobalt blue mixed with yellow ocher and white produces a subdued gray-blue which may be surprising, as you might expect a green to be the result. However, the ocher is close to orange, while the cobalt blue leans toward violet. Mixing these two almost complementary colors will always result in a gray.

RESISTS & SOLVENTS

Resist pastes or fluids can be used for decorative effect to mask out motifs or patterns. The resist is painted or sometimes sprayed onto a background paint. Once hard, it is painted over, then removed, together with the layer of paint on top, leaving the pattern in the background color. Resists can also be used for aging effects.

Modeling pastes are mixed with paint to create colored impasto or textured finishes. Normally made from a substance that gives texture, such as marbledust held together with a binder, they set very hard. They are good for stenciling three-dimensional details. You can improvize by adding whiting or sand to paint.

Solvents such as water or mineral spirits are used to dilute paint—for example, for colorwashing. Water is a solvent for latex paint, and mineral spirits for oil-based paint. For coloring a large amount of paint, thin the pigment with the solvent before adding it to the paint. However, for some techniques, you need fairly thick paint, so beware of diluting it too much.

MELTED WAX
Melt wax in a double boiler, or in a jar in a pan of boiling water, never over a naked flame, to make a resist that you can paint on.

WHITING
Resist made from whiting and water makes a rudimentary paint which, having no binder, can be wiped off when dry.

BEESWAX
Soft, bleached beeswax from an artists' supplier is ideal as a resist. It flows on smoothly and is easily removed. Spray-on beeswax allows you to tackle larger designs, but it may be hard to find. In this case, use any wax other than silicon wax. The wax must be as liquid as possible. Apply it with a cloth or sponge. The spray wax we have used is in the dish.

MODELING PASTES
This acrylic-based stucco modeling paste is quite fine. Rougher or smoother versions exist, as well as some iridescent ones.

Water or mineral spirits are the usual paint solvents. Denatured alcohol is a solvent for some wood stains and can also be used in conjunction with water-based paint to create marbling and stone finishes. For these, apply the denatured alcohol using a spray bottle. Spray bottles are also handy for spraying on water to slow down a paint's drying time. Solvents are essential, too, for cleaning brushes and equipment.

PROTECTIVE COAT

Most paint should not need protection, but painted floors or furniture might welcome a coat of wax or some layers of varnish. We prefer using wax, although it is no easy task to remove it and repaint, should you need to do so. For a really durable finish, choose an acrylic or oil-based varnish, but make sure to apply it in a dust-free atmosphere.

FINISHES
Polyurethane varnishes are very durable but slow to dry and harmful if inhaled. Acrylic varnishes do not suffer from these problems but are perhaps less durable. Wax provides a good finish. It can be applied with fine steel wool for a low sheen.

PAINTERS' TOOLS

We have a fairly ordinary collection of paintbrushes which can be used for most of our techniques. Colorwashing and stippling, for example, do not require special brushes. Large paintbrushes will do. We also use artists' brushes of varying sizes and qualities. Some recipes call for a lot of brushes. We specify one for each color. This makes for convenience, but is of course rather expensive. In most cases you can manage with far fewer brushes by washing them out and re-using them. The sizes we give are intended only as a guide. Work with what suits you and what suits the job.

Water-based paints do not brush out as well as oil-based ones. For a flat or even-textured surface we use a roller. But the cheapest means of applying paint is with a synthetic cellulose sponge. We customize these by trimming them into shapes to match the task. This also prevents them from leaving a network of straight lines in the paint. Sometimes we also use spatulas and graining tools.

BRUSHES
Among our ordinary paintbrushes are old favorites which have become worn and bristly but which still continue to perform well, and other pristine ones which remain soft and which we reserve for varnish and only varnish. Water-based paint dries quickly, so always rinse the paint out of your brushes and wash them with mild soap and water as soon as you have finished. But if you wish to continue painting within an hour or two, you can keep a loaded brush usable by wrapping it in plastic wrap.

ROLLERS AND ROCKERS

Rollers are an excellent way of applying latex paint. For small areas we sometimes apply the paint with a brush, then roller out the brush marks. We find that the most convenient rollers are the fairly small ones with push-on heads which allow for quick clean-ups and changes of color or texture as the job demands. Rollers will last as long as brushes if you care for them in the same way. Like a brush, a loaded roller can be wrapped in plastic wrap for short periods. The picture also shows a rubber graining rocker.

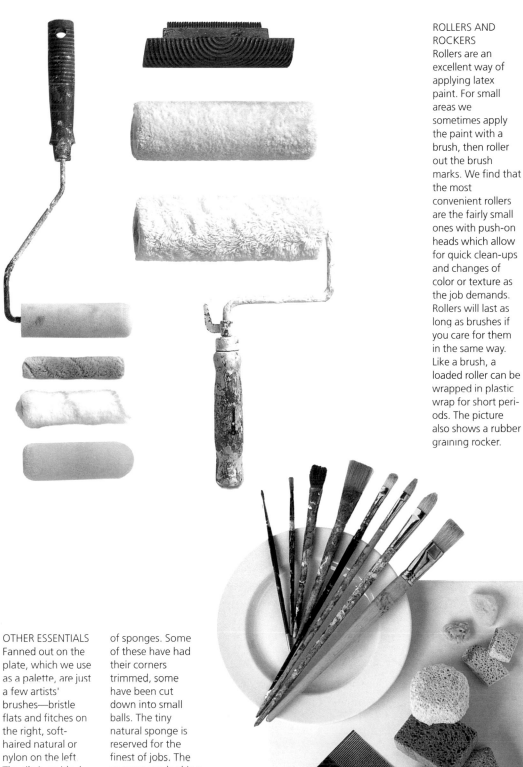

OTHER ESSENTIALS

Fanned out on the plate, which we use as a palette, are just a few artists' brushes—bristle flats and fitches on the right, soft-haired natural or nylon on the left The tile is an ideal surface for rolling paint out when you are stamping. Sitting on it are two steel decorators' combs and a bunch of sponges. Some of these have had their corners trimmed, some have been cut down into small balls. The tiny natural sponge is reserved for the finest of jobs. The anonymous-looking stick is an old brush that we use only for applying wax, and the spatula is for use with modeling pastes.

OTHER EQUIPMENT

Before you start work there is some other essential equipment you should have. For mixing large quantities of paint you will need large containers, and you should upgrade from a wooden spoon to an electric drill fitted with a paint-mixing whisk. Small amounts can be mixed in screw-top jars. Mix the paints in the jar with a long-handled brush, then put the lid on and shake furiously. If you are using powder pigments, oil-based paints, or solvents, remember that these are very toxic substances. Wear gloves and dust masks and do not smoke, eat, or drink when handling paint products.

Apart from health risks, paint can harm the environment. Protect the immediate one by spreading newspapers and drop cloths, but when disposing of solvents and unused paint, do not forget the wider one. If you first wipe and scrape as much paint as possible off equipment when cleaning up, you will need less solvent and so create less mess in your home and less damage to the environment. Dispose of solvents properly, and remember that oil-based paint and solvent-soaked rags are highly flammable.

BOWLS, KNIVES, AND SPATULAS Plastic bowls can be used to carry equipment, to mix paint in, as water reservoirs, or as dumping bins for used rags or dirty brushes. From the kitchen you will need old knives, rubber spatulas, wooden spoons, and paper towels. The only special items here are a paint roller and tray.

CONTAINERS AND PALETTES

You will need all sorts of containers and palettes. Jars are for cleaning brushes, lidded ones are for mixing and storing paint. Paint buckets are for mixing large quantities of paint for immediate use. For palettes we use saucers, plates, and ceramic tiles. When using these with acrylic colors, do not wash unused paint down the drain. Instead, let it dry on the plate, then soak off the paint film in hot water and throw it in a trash can. Clean the steel measuring spoons and plastic pitchers in the same way.

BASIC PROTECTIVE WEAR

Rubber household gloves are ideal for general tasks. For more delicate work, switch to thin latex ones. A paper mask will cut down on the inhalation of powder pigments or of dust thrown up when cleaning or sanding, but will not protect you from inhaling the harmful poisonous vapors given off by some solvents. For these you need special masks.

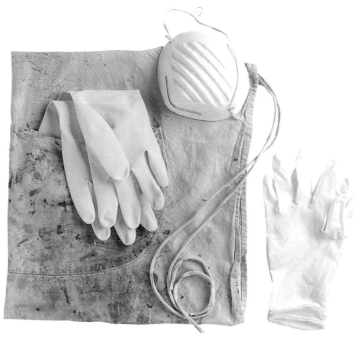

For your paintwork to look good and perform well, the surface on which it lies must be clean, free of grease, smooth, without holes or cracks, and properly primed. The chart on pages 28–9 is a guide to the treatment of both new and old materials commonly found in the home. If the surface you are working on is not listed here, seek advice in a special manual or at your local hardware store.

First you must clean off any dust or grubbiness. Detergent is often sufficient but must be properly rinsed off. Degreaser also etches the surface and provides a "key" or "tooth" for the new paint. Do not swamp bare wood, fresh plaster, or ferrous metals with water, as they will be damaged. Marks such as grease can be removed with a solvent such as mineral spirits, acetone, or denatured alcohol.

Holes, cracks, or dents must now be filled. Choose a putty to suit the surface and the size of the problem. Next, smooth the surface as flat as possible. Electric sanders produce a lot of dust and do not get into the corners. Using waterproof sand paper with water gets around the dust problem, but it cannot be used with an electric sander. Some gypsum plasters, wallboard, and wallpaper cannot be sanded at all.

Finally, most surfaces must be primed to seal and stabilize them and to ensure that they will accept the paint.

BASIC CLEANING KIT
If you are painting over previously decorated surfaces, you will need a bowl, sponge, rubber gloves, and degreaser. Alternatives to degreaser are washing soda or detergent powders. All will remove grease, but you should rinse off their residue well with plenty of clean water. Rough-textured surfaces or tough grime may also need a scrubbing brush to bring them up to scratch.

SANDING
Graded by number, sand papers range from 120 (coarse), to 600 (fine). Ordinary sand paper is cheap but clogs readily. It is good for general use. Aluminum oxide paper, the yellow paper shown here, is superior. It clogs less readily and is less scratchy. Both types are used dry and create dust, so take sensible precautions and never dry-sand lead-based paint. Silicon carbide or waterproof sand paper, also shown here, is the most versatile. Used wet, it will not clog up and does not cause dust. For flaky or rusty surfaces, you may need a wire brush, steel wool, or a pan scourer.

MECHANICAL SANDING
This will make short work of large flat areas. The small sander is easy to use, with its speed controls and disks attached by hook and loop tape. It produces an excellent finish but will not deal with curves and corners. And despite the bag, it kicks up dust.

MATERIAL	CLEAN/ DEGREASE	REPAIR/ FILL	RUB DOWN/ SAND	PRIMER	SAFETY
Wood including plywood	Can be washed, but as a general rule do not wet lumber—it will raise the grain and may cause warping.	• Spackling compound • Wood filler	• Dry-sand. Machines can speed things up. • De-nib with fine sandpaper after primer.	• Acrylic primer ⓦ • Wood primer plus stain-blocking sealer for resinous knots ⓞ	• Dust mask
Waxed wood	Very difficult to strip. Try: • mineral spirits • liquid-stripping • heat-stripping N.B. Water-based paint will not adhere to a waxy surface, so it *must* be removed.	As wood	As wood plus steel wool	As wood	
Chipboard, particleboard	• Wipe clean of dust and grime, but avoid getting too wet or they will swell and distort.	As above. Chipboard does not have a smooth texture, and spot-filling will show. Skimming the whole surface is an option if it is not a floor panel.	• Can be lightly abraded to give key for paint, but cannot be made smoother with sandpaper—only rougher. • De-nib with fine sandpaper after primer.	Can be primed with latex flat ⓦ or treat as wood.	• Dust mask
Ferrous metal e.g. steel tables	• Degrease with mineral spirits and steel wool or rag. • Brush down loose rust.	• Plastic fillers for car-body repair	• Steel wool • Sand paper used with mineral spirits • Emery cloth	• Zinc phosphate ⓞ • Red iron oxide ⓞ essential to prevent corrosion	• Dust mask • Rubber gloves
Non-ferrous metal e.g. aluminum window frames	• Degrease with mineral spirits and steel wool or rag. • Wash with detergent.	As above	• Use waterproof sand paper with water.	• Etch primers ⓞ • Zinc phosphate ⓞ • Chromate primer ⓞ	• Dust mask • Rubber gloves
Plaster	• Brush down. • Can be washed, but allow to dry out before painting, especially if using oil-based paint.	• Spackling compound • Wood putty • Plaster	• Dry • Waterproof sand paper Take care. Some plasters, e.g. gypsum, can be damaged when sanded. Others, especially plaster of Paris, can be smoothed beautifully.	• Acrylic primer ⓦ • Thinned latex flat ⓦ • Thinned white glue ⓦ • Primer-sealer ⓦ ⓞ • Alkali-resistant primer ⓞ	• Dust mask

MATERIAL	CLEAN/ DEGREASE	REPAIR/ FILL	RUB DOWN/ SAND	PRIMER	SAFETY
Wallboard, e.g. plasterboard	Usually new, so should be clean	• Spackling compound • Wood putty • Plaster	• Dry. Use very fine abrasives and sand only the filler, not the paper coating on the board.	As for plaster	
Cement on walls	• Stiff brush • Degreaser • Detergent	• Spackling compound • Cement or mortar	Not possible	• Primer-sealer ⊙ • Acrylic primer ⓦ	• Rubber gloves
on floors	• Stiff brush • Degreaser • Detergent	• Cement or mortar	Not needed	• Stabilizing solution ⊙	• Rubber gloves
Previously painted surfaces	• Degreaser • Detergent • Mineral spirits	Depends on what lies below. Spackling compound will suit most circumstances, or use filler specific to plaster, wood, metal, etc.	• Dry • Waterproof sand paper on sound paint and on nonabsorbent foundations • If foundation shows through, treat accordingly. Paint may be stripped with liquid stripper or burned off.	On sound surfaces no primer may be needed. If in doubt, use acrylic primer or oil undercoat. If foundation shows through, spot-prime with appropriate primer.	• Dust mask • Rubber gloves, mask, and goggles
Papered walls	If unsound, strip off completely and treat support accordingly. It will probably be plaster. If sound, wipe clean.	• Spackling compound • Wood putty	No—except dry-sand filler.	• Acrylic primer ⓦ	
Varnished surfaces	Treat as previously painted surfaces.	Treat as previously painted surfaces.	Treat as previously painted surfaces.	Treat as previously painted surfaces.	
Laminates and plastics	• Degreaser • Detergent • Mineral spirits	• Plastic fillers for car-body repair	• Waterproof sand paper • Coarse emery cloth	• Oil primer, e.g. metal primer, followed by acrylic primer if using water-based paint	• Rubber gloves
Glass	• Detergent • Glass paint solvent • Denatured alcohol				
New cork tiles				None	
Old varnished cork tiles	• Detergent • Degreaser		• Sand lightly • Steel wool	None	

w = water-based   o = oil-based

STENCILS

Essential equipment for making stencils are a craft or X-Acto knife and a cutting mat. Access to a photocopier will save you from having to trace and transfer. Stencils can be cut from cardboard, paper, or plastic. If they are to be used repeatedly, we use oiled manila stencil board. The oil makes the board more durable and also easier to cut.

Photocopy the image you want at the size you want, then glue it to your stencil board using repositionable spray adhesive. Repeat patterns will be a lot easier to line up and register if you place your image at the center of a square or rectangular board. Cut through both photocopy and board with the knife. Be firm, and try to cut in a single stroke. For a softer edge, tear the shape out instead of cutting it. We sometimes use an acetate sheet. This has the advantage that you are able to photocopy a design directly onto it.

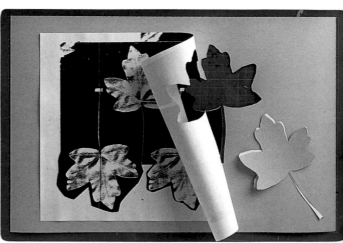

MATERIALS FOR STENCILS
Top left is a stencil torn from oiled manila paper, and alongside it, one that has been cut with a knife. Images need be nothing more than photocopies of leaves, held in place on the stencil board with repositionable spray adhesive, then cut through to make the stencil. Use masking tape to mark the positions of your stencils on the wall, and spray adhesive to hold them in place without damaging the surface while you stencil. Take great care when using spray adhesive. It is extremely toxic.

2 With the stencil still in place, sponge in a second color along the bottom edge and partway up the side. Once most of the paint has left the sponge, start moving the sponge up the motif to form a shadow, its color fading away gradually. Add some of the same color to the stalk also.

1 Hold the stencil in place with spray adhesive. Have ready a spoonful of acrylic paint on a saucer, and a piece of trimmed cellulose sponge. Dip the sponge into the paint, but do not overload it. Gently dab the color into the stencil. Aim for all-over distribution of the paint, but don't be too worried about achieving an even texture.

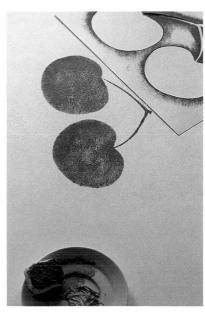

3 Once the stenciling is completed, peel away the stencil, and allow to dry.

4 You will be left with a pair of gently shaded cherries.

S T A M P S

MATERIALS FOR STAMPS
Foam rubber is cut to shape and glued to a backing board with paper cement. For complex shapes, trace the design onto paper, cut it out, and use as a template to draw around with a fine waterproof marker. For a mosaic effect, make stamps from small pieces of foam rubber glued to a backing board. For a two-color motif, use two interlocking stamps, as shown here.

Stamps are a quicker way of applying designs than stencils and are ideal for small, uncomplicated motifs. Most of our stamps are made from thin, foam-rubber mat of the kind hikers carry. This is very easy to cut and holds its shape well, while being elastic enough to print on top of uneven surfaces. You can also make stamps from the flocked draining mats used for wine glasses. Experiment with whatever is available; you may discover an interesting new effect.

Cut your design using an X-Acto knife. Work on a cutting mat to do this. The stamp must then be stuck to a backing board which should remain rigid and not warp when wet. Foamcore board, available from art supply stores, is quick and easy to cut. You may also use scraps of wood. These are cheaper and have the advantage that you can screw handles or knobs to their backs, which makes the stamping process considerably easier.

Much smaller stamps can be carved from an eraser, using an X-Acto knife. If you can't find an eraser big enough, glue four together with extra-strong glue. These will not need a backing board.

When you are cutting your stamps, don't forget that you are making a mirror-image. Getting the motif the wrong way around may not be too serious for many of the projects in this book, but if you intend to stamp any lettering, make sure you get it right.

1 To apply the paint to small stamps, use a roller to spread the paint onto a tile, then press the stamp into the paint. Reload the stamp with paint for each print.

2 Place the stamp in position along a guideline, which can be masking tape, as here, or a stretched-out string; then press down firmly. The wooden backing board is thick enough for you to grip comfortably with your fingers.

1 This larger stamp has the paint applied to it directly with a roller. The roller is made of sponge covered in flock and was originally designed for painting behind radiators.

2 Test your stamp on a piece of paper before you start work to make sure that you are applying pressure equally to all sections of the motif.

MASKING OUT

We find masking tape indispensable. Because it does not stick permanently to a surface, it can be used in all sorts of ways—holding stencils in place, attaching color swatches and sketches to a wall, marking height lines and center lines, and so on.

It is sold in several forms. The ordinary type is good for masking off windows, floors, and all those fixtures that you would otherwise have to paint around very carefully. Mostly though, we use it within a design to prevent paint from drifting into areas where we don't want it to go, or to create stripes or the sharp edges of a shape. However, ordinary tape can pull off a paint film if it is very fresh or has been applied to a poorly prepared surface. Manufacturers now make tapes for delicate or freshly painted surfaces, but test them in an unobtrusive place before pressing them into service. Another special tape is one that will follow a curve (see page 36).

Some techniques and projects require you to mask off well beyond the shape you are working on. This can be done by gluing cash register tape alongside thin tape, rather than by buying a wide tape. You can use double-sided masking tape which makes this very easy to do.

Cash register tape and paper can also be turned into masking with the aid of repositionable spray adhesive. And tape and paper can all be torn to give a softer edge to a design rather than the super-straight edge that you usually get with tapes.

MASKING TAPES
This selection of masking materials includes masking tape that can follow a curve, as well as a blue safe-release tape for use on delicate surfaces. The tape for delicate surfaces is very flat, allowing almost no seepage of paint underneath if it is well applied. Cash register tape and ordinary parcel paper can also be used for masks.

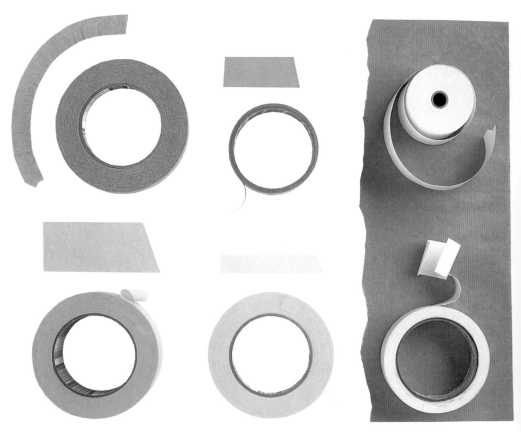

 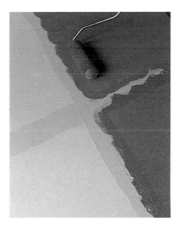 

1 Tear cash register tape along its length, spray it with repositionable spray adhesive, and use to mask out a cross.

2 Apply the paint using a small roller, taking care that you do not press too hard and force paint under the masking.

3 Slowly peel the masking away. The uneven edges left by the torn tape give a soft, natural look.

  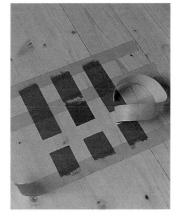

1 Lay out a grid of masking tape, pressing it down well, then sponge undiluted color into the squares.

2 With careful sponging, it is possible to paint individual squares in different colors.

3 Once the paint is touch-dry, peel the tape away to reveal a crisp-edged motif.

1 Use a combination of cash register tape and masking tape to mask off alternate stripes on a colorwashed background, then apply a second color using a roller.

2 Wait until the paint is touch-dry, then carefully peel off the masking to reveal colorwashed stripes.

MORE MASKING OUT

Masking can also be used to draw and shade motifs. Ordinary masking tape can easily be torn along its length, and strips of torn tape can be built up into attractive, angular motifs. Flexible masking tape can be used for curvilinear designs. It may be difficult to find, and in some cases ⅛in. (3mm.)–wide Fineline tape can be substituted in conjunction with regular masking tape. Use the Fineline tape to mask the curved edges. Secure it down, to prevent paint from spilling over, with short lengths of regular masking tape; you can clip into these to get around the curves. Make sure both tapes are well stuck down.

1 Tear small strips of tape along their length and stick them down in a spiral with their ragged edge facing outward.

2 Use more tape and cash register tape to mask off a square around the spiral. Apply the color using a small roller.

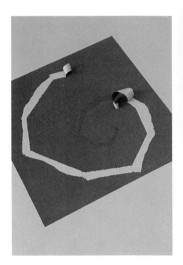

3 Once the paint is touch-dry, carefully remove all the masking to leave behind an angular spiral on a square. You could "tile" a whole floor in this way.

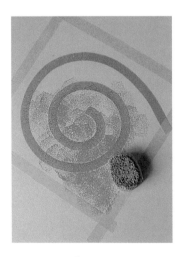

1 Stick flexible masking tape firmly down on a line drawn with water-soluble marker. Mask off a square around the spiral. Sponge the color on lightly with dryish paint.

2 When the paint is touch-dry, slowly remove the tape.

3 Remove the rest of the masking, and you will be left with a spiral design on a square.

1 Mask off a square. Sponge lightly all over in red, then use a torn strip of stencil board to mask across the diagonal. Sponge again in red on one side of the diagonal.

2 Use another torn strip of stencil board to mask across the other diagonal, and sponge lightly in blue.

3 Using both strips together across the diagonals, sponge in the final section in a solid blue.

4 Your finished result will appear to be a pyramid with each face illuminated in a slightly different manner.

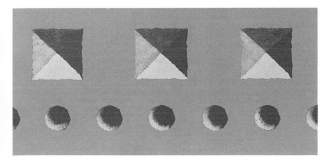

5 This technique was used to make the stenciled border on page 71.

PLANNING

A little forethought will enable you to carry out your ideas effectively. If you are working on a large wall or floor, take a good look at it and note the position of any architectural details—for instance doors and windows—that will have to be included in your design. Consider such things as the height of your proposed border in relation to windows, the positions of light fixtures and electrical outlets if you are contemplating stripes on your wall, or how to fit a repeat pattern across a chimney breast without risking ending up with incomplete motifs at either side.

It may help to sketch your design out on graph paper. If you work in standard measurements, you should use a scale of 1:12. If you work in metric measurements a scale of 1:10 is handy, as 1 meter is represented as 10cm., or 100mm. With a scale of 1:10, a wall 3.2 x 2.7m. (10 x 9ft.) would be drawn to about the size of these two pages.

This same wall is 90ft.[2] (8.6m.[2]). A quart of latex flat paint can usually cover up to 150ft.[2] (14m.[2]), so if the wall includes a window or a door, you will be able to coat it twice, but it all depends on the thickness of the paint and the absorbency and texture of the wall. Cans of paint and primer usually carry information on coverage, so take a list of dimensions to the store. Our recipes specify what area they will cover.

EQUIPMENT FOR PLANNING
Once you have chosen your motif, you must plan your design. Plenty of graph paper, a long ruler, right-angled triangle, pencils, and a calculator are the basic kit you will need. Once you have drawn a scale plan that fits, you will be ready to mark it out on the surface you are decorating.

As you work, you will need to mark your surface with center lines, horizontals, and registration marks. If these are not to be covered by paint, they must be temporary. Masking tape is useful for this, as it can be written on. Water-soluble markers are also handy since the marks they make can be wiped off most non-absorbent surfaces. As a precaution, though, use a marker that matches your paint.

To rule long, straight lines, stretch out a length of string, securing it with nails or masking tape. Or use a builders' chalk line. Stretch its chalky string tightly between two points and pluck it to snap a line on floor or wall. Horizontals and verticals can be ruled with a level at least 3ft. (1m.) long. But there is also the school of thought that says you must line up designs with floors and ceilings, even if these are not completely straight, and we would not disagree with that. If the layout looks right, go ahead and start painting.

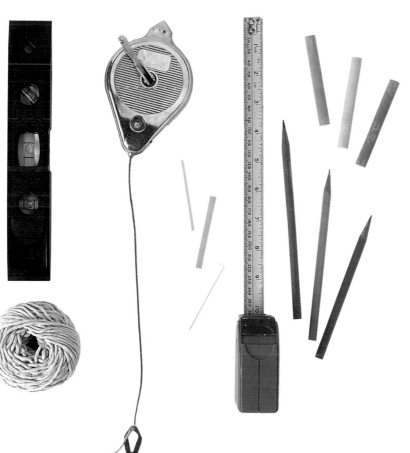

EQUIPMENT FOR MARKING
Tautly stretched string makes an excellent guide which won't harm the surface, nor will the builders' chalk line which doubles as a plumb line. If you have to draw on your surface, choose pencils for a wooden surface, and artists' water-soluble markers for non-absorbent ones. Chalks are good for tracing and for rough layouts. All can be erased or wiped off.

CARPENTER'S LEVEL
A small level can be useful in tight spots, but this longer one is best when ruling a horizontal or a vertical.

PART TWO

TECHNIQUES

An introduction to the techniques you will need for applying both paint and pattern, together with ideas on how to incorporate them into simple and effective designs in a variety of colors.

An example of what can be achieved using a combination of techniques. The fossil set in granite (see pages 179–81) is made by combining stone effects, stenciling, and a whiting resist. The result is an elegant and unusual table top.

TECHNIQUES

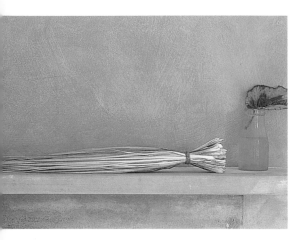

The techniques you will need for applying your paint lie at the heart of all the project and design ideas in this book. In the following pages we explain all the principal techniques that we use. These are simply ways of applying and manipulating paint to create a range of surface textures, from flat matte to highly decorative. They include techniques such as colorwashing, dry brushing, and sponging, as well as finishes you can develop from these—for instance, creating stone effects, a variation of sponging off.

To these paint techniques we have added stamping, stenciling, and the use of masking and resists—all methods of producing and/or reproducing a design in a controlled manner. Stamping and stenciling allow you to apply a motif—repeatedly if you want—to a surface. Masks and resists prevent paint from going into one area while you are working on another. At their most basic, masking and resists are essential if you do not want all-over pattern or texture. But they can be used to add a decorative element in their own right. For instance, strips of torn paper can mask off a shape so that once paint is applied and the masking removed, the shape remains in the original color.

All of our techniques are very simple. None requires special knowledge or expensive equipment and they can usually be mastered quickly. In the case of the stencils and stamps, we have kept our designs simple so they are easy to cut and apply. We have aimed to use all our techniques in a way that gives a great deal of freedom, providing a result that looks fresh and contemporary.

Gaining confidence in handling your materials and equipment is all part of the pleasure of decorating. There is no doubt that the best way to do this is to practice as much as possible. Use an area

Left: Color-washing is an especially useful technique which can stand on its own—as does this beautiful blue-green wash above a fireplace—or work in partnership with a pattern or motif.

Below: Here checks are set out in a diamond pattern to make an effect reminiscent of an Amish quilt hanging on the wall. But touches of gold stamped on some of the diamonds pick up the hand-painted gold of the bed and the gold of the curtains to create an altogether more opulent look.

Left: Painting old beams with a leopard-skin effect may seem an irreverent way to treat them, but remember paint does not have to be permanent. When the owner of this room has tired of the "Out of Africa" look, it can easily be changed.

of wall that can be painted over afterward, or scraps of wallboard, which is what we used for many of the examples here. These have the extra advantage that you can pick them up and move them around, since colors will change their appearance in different lights and according to their position in a room.

Choice of color and of design are all very personal matters. No one can tell you what to like or what will suit your particular room or life style. You can only learn through observation, and still more observation. That is why this book is full of so many different design and project ideas, all worked in several different color schemes. Even the basic techniques are shown in alternative color combinations, as well as with some additional decorative device—whether to manipulate them into stripes or panels, or to add a masked-out motif.

Above: There is much to be admired in traditional stencils like these by Lyn le Grice, but they can be complex to cut and use. For a contemporary interior, a simpler, more abstract motif would be an alternative.

If you like what you see here, you can incorporate it immediately in your own decorating. Otherwise, you could take one technique—say rubbing off—and use it as the background to a stenciled or stamped design. Or, if you like a technique, but not our choice of colors, experiment using a color recipe from elsewhere in the book. We hope we have provided you with a starting point. The rest is up to you.

COLORWASHING

This is one of the most useful techniques. A single glaze can be an effective treatment for a wall, leaving a broken surface, as opposed to the flat, single-toned finish that results from a roller. If you apply several layers of glaze, the surface becomes richer and multi-toned. Brush marks disappear under each successive glaze coat, leaving a soft, gently textured surface.

The wall you are to work on should be well prepared and white. High-quality latex flat paints are ideal as a base. Cheaper latex paints may have chalk or whiting as a pigment, which makes them too absorbent, so the glaze cannot be moved around on it.

The colorwash dries quickly, so if you are tackling a large surface, it would be a good idea to have two people working together. The glazing liquid in the colorwash mix helps to extend slightly the glaze's drying time, so making it a little easier to manipulate. It also gives the glaze a slightly harder finish.

We have made much use of colorwashing throughout this book, either as a background to the motifs, or for the motifs themselves. Here we show how it can be used by itself to stripe a wall. In two of our samples, the two glazes we use are the same color. This enriches the first glaze and brings it down a tone. In the other two samples, the second glaze is a different but similar color. This creates a more complex and subtle surface. If you opt to use a second color that is from a different part of the spectrum than the first, you will not end up with such subtlety of color; however, this should not stop you from experimenting if you wish.

The recipes are for a wall approximately 54ft.^{2} (5m.^{2})

COLORWASHED STRIPES

INGREDIENTS **See swatch captions.**

EQUIPMENT **Medium-textured paint roller plus tray / 1 or 2 large containers/ 2 or 4 x 4in. (100mm.) paintbrushes / rags/ tape measure / straightedge / water-soluble marker or chalk line / safe-release masking tape / cash register tape**

INSTRUCTIONS 1 Prepare the surface thoroughly. See pages 26–9.
2 Use a medium-textured paint roller to apply two coats of white latex flat paint to the wall. You should be aiming to create a surface which is free of brush strokes but has a slight texture. Leave 4 hours to dry between coats, and 24 hours after the second coat to make a really hard surface ready for the next stage.
3 Mix your glaze or glazes in one or more containers.
4 Load one of the paintbrushes with glaze, and apply to a

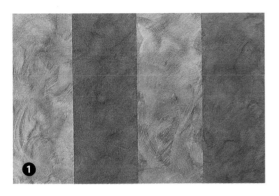

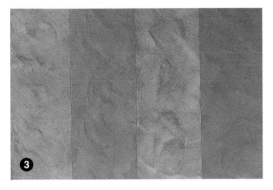

❶ BLUE ON BLUE
On a base of 1qt. (1 liter) white latex flat, a mixture of 3tbsp. white latex flat, 1½tsp. quin-acridone violet, 6tbsp. ultra-marine plus 5oz. (150ml.) acrylic glazing liquid and 20oz. (600ml.) water will colorwash the wall twice.

❸ DULL TURQUOISE GREEN ON BLUE
On the same base coat, apply a first glaze of swatch 1 colorwash, and a second glaze of 3tbsp. white latex flat, 3tbsp. cobalt blue, 2tsp. yellow ocher, 3½oz. (100ml.) acrylic glazing liquid, and 13½oz. (400ml.) water.

section of the wall. Brush it on in all directions in quick, curving, random strokes. Almost immediately, follow up with the clean, dry paintbrush. Skim the second brush over the paint in all directions until you reach the point where the brush begins to drag and starts to lift the paint off rather than moving it around. Now you should work a little more firmly. Aim to soften all the brush strokes, but do not worry if some remain stronger than others. That is all part of the desired effect. The paint will be completely dry in only a matter of seconds.

5 Move quickly on to the next section of the wall, and repeat the process. The second brush will become wet as you work, so you will need to dry it off frequently on a rag. Repeat the process until you have completed the wall. Leave to dry at least 4 hours.

6 Use the tape measure, straightedge, and crayon to measure and mark out a series of 8in. (20cm.) stripes (see page 39). Mask out alternate stripes with masking tape and cash register tape (see pages 34–5). Take care when applying masking tape to the freshly painted areas. If possible, use a safe-release masking tape.

7 Use the paintbrushes to apply the second glaze coat in the same manner as the first. Remove all the masking, and allow to dry (4 hours).

❷ BEIGE ON BEIGE
Again on a base coat of 1qt. (1 liter) white latex flat, a mixture of 7½tbsp. white and 3tbsp. raw sienna mixed with 5oz. (150ml.) acrylic glazing liquid and 20oz. (600ml.) water will colorwash the wall twice.

❹ BROWN ON BEIGE
On the same base coat, apply a first glaze of swatch 2 colorwash, and a second of 2tbsp. white latex flat, 4tbsp. burnt sienna, and 1½tsp. dioxazine purple, 3½oz. (100ml.) acrylic glazing liquid, and 13½oz. (400ml.) water.

DRY BRUSHING

Dry brushing is similar in many ways to colorwashing, but the overall effect is softer. In dry brushing the brush is not fully loaded with paint which means that runs, splashes, dribbles, and seepage beneath masking tape are not usually a problem. The technique of dry brushing, however, requires some vigor, so we normally apply only a single coat, and we also work in small, contained areas.

On pages 92–5, we have used dry brushing to paint the vertical bands of color over which we printed the squiggle motifs. Here we show that dividing a wall into panels of color not only gives you a means to manage the technique but also provides a discreet and easy-to-achieve design for a wall.

As with colorwashing, your base coat should be high-quality white latex flat paint. Our standard recipe for dry brushing is 1 part color : 1 part glazing liquid : 2 parts water, but it can be varied by using less or no water. Dark colors require the most water to lighten them, whereas pale colors work better with less. You should also take into account the quality of your paint. If it is thin and watery to begin with, you will have to reduce the amount of water. Check the consistency by doing a trial run on a scrap of plasterboard or on an area of wall which is due to be painted out afterward.

These recipes are for a wall approximately 65ft.^{2} (6m.^{2}).

DRY-BRUSHED PANELS

INGREDIENTS

See swatch captions.

EQUIPMENT

Medium-textured paint roller plus tray / tape measure / straightedge / water-soluble marker or chalk line / safe-release masking tape / cash register tape or clean paper / container / 1 x 4in. (100mm.) paintbrush / ceramic tile

INSTRUCTIONS

1 Prepare the surface thoroughly. See pages 26–9.

2 Use a medium-textured paint roller to apply two coats of white latex flat paint to the wall. You should be aiming to create a surface that is free of brush strokes but has a slight texture. Allow 4 hours to dry between coats, and 24 hours after the second coat.

3 Using the tape measure, straightedge, and marker, mark the wall into panels 22–43ft.^{2} (2–4m.^{2}). The exact size will be governed by the size of your wall. Using the masking tape, mask off as many alternate panels as possible, extending the width of the masking with cash register tape or clean paper (see pages 34–5).

4 Mix the glaze coat in the container, then dab the tips of the paintbrush into the glaze. Only a little is needed. Stipple the

❶ **EMERALD GREEN**
Over a base coat of 1qt. (1liter) white latex flat paint, we applied an emerald green glaze made from 4tbsp. phthalo-cyanine green and 3tbsp. yellow ocher added to 4oz. (120ml.) white latex flat. The yellow ocher takes some of the sharpness out of the green. The color was mixed with 7½oz. (225ml.) acrylic glazing liquid, and up to 17oz. (500ml.) water.

❷ **TERRACOTTA**
With the same base coat as swatch 1, we used a glaze made from 5½oz. (160ml.) pimento red latex flat, to which we added 8tsp. burnt sienna and 4tsp. white. The burnt sienna helps give the color a more antique look. The color was mixed with 7½oz. (220ml.) acrylic glazing liquid and up to 15oz. (450ml.) water.

❸ **DOVE GRAY**
The simplest recipe and the most subtle. On the same base coat as described previously, apply a glaze made from 6¾oz. (200ml.) white latex flat paint and 1tbsp. black artists' acrylic color, mixed with 7¼oz. (215ml.) acrylic glazing liquid and up to 15oz. (450ml.) water.

brush on the tile to distribute the paint evenly across the bristles. Starting at the top of a panel, brush the paint out in all directions. You can also use a rubbing action. The paint will spread out into a softly textured layer with many variations in tone. Do not overwork the glaze, or you may start to rub it off.

5 Once you have used up the glaze on your brush, dip it into the glaze again, stipple it on the tile, and continue down the panel. You must work briskly in order to successfully blend one section with the next. As you proceed, you will see the wisdom of dividing the wall up into small, manageable areas.

6 Complete each of the masked-off panels in turn, then remove the masking tape. Leave to dry for 2 hours to ensure that the glaze is not disturbed at the next stage.

7 Mask off another set of panels and repeat. Take care when applying masking tape to the freshly painted areas. If possible, use a tape designed for delicate surfaces. Remove the masking and allow to dry (2 hours).

Continue like this until all the panels have been completed. The soft checkerboard effect will appear as a result of slight variations in the color and texture that are typical of this technique.

RUBBING OFF

This is a fairly straightforward technique which gives an aged texture to a freshly painted surface by rubbing away some of the paint before it has completely dried. We have used it in combination with a stencil, which allowed us to paint and age a series of small motifs without affecting the previously painted surroundings.

Unlike most of our stenciling, in this project an ordinary paintbrush was used to apply the paint, since a thick layer is necessary to achieve the desired result. You will also need a strong arm!

The recipes are for a wall approximately 54–65ft.^{2} (5–6m.^{2}).

RUBBED PITCHERS

INGREDIENTS

See swatch captions.

EQUIPMENT

Container / paint roller plus tray / tracing paper / pencil / paper / stencil board / X-Acto knife / cutting mat / repositionable spray adhesive / tape measure / straightedge / water-soluble marker / screw-top jar / 1 x 2in. (50mm.) paintbrush / rag / bowl of water / 2 cellulose sponges

INSTRUCTIONS

1 Prepare the surface thoroughly. See pages 26–9.
2 Mix the background color in the container. Use the paint roller to apply two coats to the surface to be decorated, allowing 4 hours to dry between coats.
3 Trace the design on page 182, enlarge it on a photocopier, and use it to make the pitcher stencil (see page 30). Keep the loose piece of stencil board from the handle. In our design, the pitcher is 8in. (20cm.) high and 10in. (25cm.) wide.
4 Use the tape measure, straightedge, and marker to mark out the positions of each pitcher. Our spacing is 8in. (20cm.) between motifs in all directions.
5 Spray the back of the stencil with adhesive and lay it in its first position. Spray the loose piece of stencil board and position it to make the handle.
6 Mix the pitcher color in the screw-top jar, and use the brush to stencil in the pitcher. Apply the paint carefully, brushing away from the stencil edge or along it, but never toward it, to prevent bleeding.
7 Remove the stencil, and repeat for two or three more motifs. Leave the paint to dry for 10–15 minutes.
8 Soak the rag in water, wring it out, and use it to rub at the fresh paint. Some of the paint will be removed quite quickly, and if, like us, you rub hard enough, you will remove some of the background color as well, so creating highlights on your

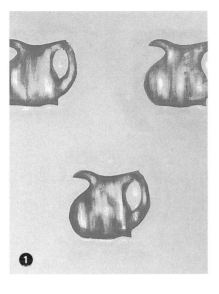

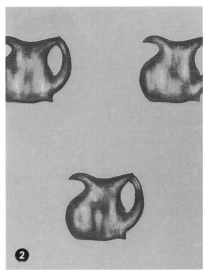

❷ SMOKY PURPLE ON SOFT YELLOW
Here the background uses a mixture of 13½oz. (400ml.) white latex flat with 4tbsp. yellow ocher. The pitchers are 4tbsp. white latex flat, with 4tsp. dioxazine purple, 2tsp. ultramarine, and 1tsp. black.

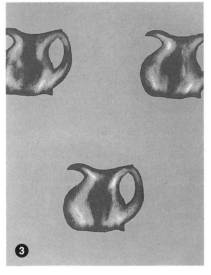

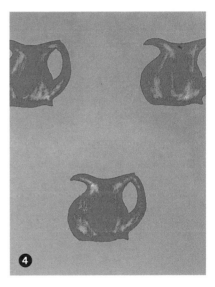

❶ GREEN ON LILAC
In this color choice, the background was a mixture of 15oz. (450ml.) white latex flat, with 3tbsp. neutral gray and 2tsp. dioxazine purple. The pitchers were stenciled in 3tbsp. white latex flat, mixed with 8tsp. raw umber and 4tsp. phthalocyanine green.

❸ ORANGE ON GRAY GREEN
This background is 13½oz. (400ml.) white latex flat, with 5tbsp. cobalt blue and 8tsp. yellow ocher. The pitchers use 4tbsp. yellow ocher, mixed with 3tbsp. white and 2tsp. naphthol red.

pitchers where the undercoat shines through. As you work, you should wash the cloth out frequently in water and continually clean up around the edges of the pitchers using a clean sponge.

If, before rubbing off, you leave the paint to dry for slightly longer than the 10–15 minutes stated in the instructions, you will find that it will be more difficult to remove. The result will be that less paint will come off and the finished effect will be slightly different. On the other hand, the rubbing off itself is less messy, and it is easier to clean up around the motifs.

9 Repeat the process for all the other pitchers. Finally, clean the whole surface with a large clean sponge and fresh water, and leave to dry for a few hours.

❹ COBALT BLUE ON GRAY
This background is 1pt. (480ml.) white latex flat paint, mixed with 1tbsp. black artists' acrylic color, while the pitchers are stenciled with 5tbsp. cobalt blue and 5tsp. white latex flat. In this color scheme, we left the paint to dry for longer, so less was removed.

SPONGING

There is a wide range of natural and synthetic sponges on the market that you can use for sponging. You should experiment, as each will give a different finish. In the following recipes we use standard cellulose sponges. The amount of paint applied with a sponge can differ, too, leaving you with a range of possibilities from a solid, opaque finish to a light, open texture which allows the color below to show through.

SPONGING ON

Sponging on is our standard method of applying paint for stenciling. It is also a quick and easy way of giving a texture to a surface—for example, the granular texture on our counter front on pages 100–103. This recipe will cover an area approximately 54ft^2. (5m.^{2}).

INGREDIENTS

See swatch captions.

EQUIPMENT

Paint roller plus tray / 3 cellulose sponges / scissors / 3 screw-top jars / 3 large plates / tape measure / safe-release masking tape / cash register tape

INSTRUCTIONS

1 Prepare the surface thoroughly. See pages 26–9.

2 Use the roller to apply two coats of white latex flat paint, allowing each coat to dry (4 hours).

3 Squared-off sponges can leave lines in the paint, so trim them into a rounded shape with scissors.

4 Mix each of the sponging colors in a screw-top jar, and spoon some of the first color onto a plate. Dip your sponge into it, then pat it up and down for a moment to spread the paint evenly across the surface of the sponge. If you feel you have too much on your sponge, pat it on the plate a little longer. To create the lightly textured effect that is required here, the holes in the sponge should not be filled with paint.

5 Use a light dabbing motion to sponge the paint on. Try to vary the action as you work, or you may find that you are building up a pattern that is too repetitious. Complete the sponging in this manner, reloading your sponge with paint at regular intervals. Allow to dry (2–4 hours).

6 Use masking tape and cash register tape to mask off an 8in. (20cm.)-wide band (see pages 34–5). Sponge in the same way with the second sponging color. Remove the masking and allow to dry (2–4 hours).

7 Mask off the second band in the same way, and sponge in the third color. Remove the masking and allow to dry. The final effect is similar in appearance to a woven fabric such as gingham or madras cotton.

SPONGING

❶ BLUE GREEN AND DARK GRAY OVER CREAMY YELLOW
Here the base coat is 1qt. (1 liter) white latex flat, with a first sponged coat of 17oz. (500ml.) white latex flat mixed with 2tsp. cadmium yellow, 2tsp. yellow ocher, and 1tsp. neutral gray. The second sponged coat is 8tsp. white latex flat with 6tbsp. black and 2tbsp. burnt umber. The third is 5½tbsp. white latex flat, 5½tbsp. cobalt blue, and 4tsp. yellow ocher.

❷ BLUE GRAY AND PEACH OVER LILAC
With the same base coat as in swatch 1, the first sponged coat is 15oz. (450ml.) white latex flat mixed with 1tbsp. neutral gray and 2tsp. dioxazine purple. The second sponged coat consists of 5oz. (150ml.) white latex flat mixed with 2tbsp. ultramarine, while the third sponged coat is 5tbsp. white latex flat mixed with 3½oz. (100ml.) yellow ocher and 1tbsp. naphthol red.

SPONGING OFF

This technique is an essential part of the stone finishes on pages 64–5, it provided the backgrounds to the tables on pages 172–5, and gave the texture to the stripe on pages 108–10. We also use the technique to modify a motif's texture, as when we pressed a clean, damp sponge onto the freshly painted border of the cabinets on pages 148–51

With sponging off, paint is applied to a surface, then some is lifted off with a wet or damp sponge. If you splash, spray, or sprinkle water onto the paint as it dries, it will soften in those places, and this paint will lift off more readily. Open, more vigorously textured sponging off requires a lot of water, so can only successfully be carried out on a horizontal surface. On walls, use spray bottles and wet sponges.

For an area such as the top of a small table, you will need only about two or three tablespoons of color, depending on the texture you want. This recipe will cover an area approximately 32ft.² (3m.²).

INGREDIENTS See swatch captions (over).

EQUIPMENT Paint roller plus tray / 2 large plates / 1 x 3in. (75mm.) paintbrush / bowl of water / spray bottle (optional) / 2 or 3 cellulose sponges / paper / scissors / repositionable spray adhesive

SPONGING

1 Prepare the surface thoroughly. See pages 26–9.

2 Use the roller to apply two coats of white latex flat paint, allowing each coat 2–4 hours to dry .

3 Now work in sections no larger than 11ft.^{2} (1m.^{2}). Mix the sponging color on a plate, and apply it loosely with the paintbrush. Alternatively, you can sponge it on, but work quickly and avoid letting the paint dry out, especially at the edges. Maintaining a wet edge is essential if you are to blend one area successfully into another.

4 While the paint is still wet, splash and sprinkle water on its surface, or use a spray bottle. Leave for a moment, then dab at the surface with the sponge to pick up the paint from the wet areas. Rinse your sponge out frequently.

5 Repeat step 4 a number of times, according to how much paint you would like left behind and how much texturing you want. You will discover that differing textures can be created by varying the timing between painting and splashing, and splashing and dabbing. The amount of water you use will also have an influence on the finish.

6 Once you have a surface you are pleased with, leave it to dry for a couple of hours.

7 For the motif, cut a wobbly-edged moon from paper and attach it to the sponged surface with spray adhesive.

8 Spoon some of the glaze color onto a plate, and dip a barely damp sponge into it. Rub this evenly over the surface until you are left with a thin, transparent layer over the sponging. Remove the paper mask and allow to dry. The colored glaze gives the sponging a remarkable richness and extravagant coloring.

❶ MAGENTA OVER PRUSSIAN GREEN
With a base coat of 4oz. (125ml.) white latex flat, the sponged color is 2tbsp. Payne's gray and 2tbsp. phthalo-cyanine green, while the glaze is 2tbsp. magenta.

❷ MAGENTA OVER CADMIUM YELLOW
The base coat is as swatch 1. Replacing the Prussian green with 4tbsp. cadmium yellow changes the mood completely. The 2tbsp. magenta glaze converts the yellow into intensely rich and varied pinks.

GRAINING

Graining is done with a rubber tool called a rocker. When pulled through wet paint with a smooth, slow, rocking motion, it leaves behind a surprisingly accurate wood-grain pattern. You will probably like to practice a little first on a scrap of plywood or plasterboard.

These recipes will cover an area approximately 32–43ft.^{2} (3–4m.^{2}).

GRAINED BANDS

INGREDIENTS

See swatch captions.

EQUIPMENT

2 containers / paint roller plus tray / tape measure / straightedge / water-soluble marker / masking tape / cash register tape / screw-top jar / 1 x 3in. (75mm.) paintbrush / graining rocker / rags

INSTRUCTIONS

1 Prepare the surface thoroughly. See pages 26–9.

2 Mix the base color in a container. Use the roller to apply two coats, allowing 2–4 hours for each coat to dry.

3 Measure and mark out the surface into 12in. (30cm.) squares, using a tape measure, straightedge, and marker. Divide each square into three equal bands as shown below, and mask out as many alternate bands as possible with masking tape and cash register tape (see pages 34–5).

4 Mix the graining color and brush it on three or four masked-off bands. Drag the rocker slowly through the paint, pulling it toward you and gradually and smoothly changing its angle. You can vary the graining by altering your speed, as well as by graining with the rocker facing the opposite way. As you work, wipe excess paint from the face of the rocker.

5 Continue in the same way down each band, aiming for variety from band to band, but maintaining a family likeness between them all.

6 Remove the masking and allow to dry (2–4 hours).

7 Mask off another set of bands, and grain these in the same way. Continue until the design is complete.

❶ VIBRANT PINK OVER ACID YELLOW
All the paints used are artists' acrylic colors. For the base coat you will need 8½oz. (240ml.) cadmium yellow, 4oz. (120ml.) white, and 4oz. (120ml.) raw umber, while the graining requires 10oz. (300ml.) white, 3½oz. (100ml.) naphthol red, and 3½oz. (100ml.) vermilion.

❷ TURQUOISE OVER ACID GREEN
All the paints are artists' acrylic colors. The base coat is 17oz. (500ml.) Hansa yellow light with 1tbsp. ultramarine. Over this the graining is 8½oz. (240ml.) white, 4oz. (120ml.) phthalocyanine green, and 4oz. (120ml.) phthalocyanine blue.

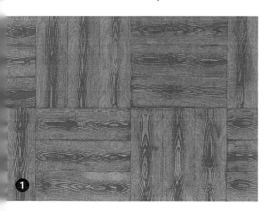

❶

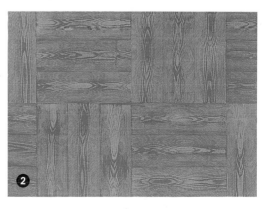

❷

AGING PAINT

Well-applied fresh paint looks beautiful. In an older house, though, it can look out of place, so you may want to create an aged finish that appears to have been around for a while. Aging is also used as a decorative finish, most commonly on wooden surfaces such as cabinet fronts, paneling, or tables, but also on walls and floors.

When paint ages, its surface starts to wear away or flakes drop off. In addition, the paint begins to acquire a patina and shine in places where it is frequently handled. For your aging to appear authentic, follow examples of genuinely aged paintwork. The following techniques show how you can achieve a similar look.

RUBBING BACK

You can use steel wool, with or without wax, to give a gently aged look to paintwork. As you rub with the steel wool, you will break through the paint to reveal the surface below. If you use the steel wool with wax, you must be certain that you do not plan to apply more coats of paint, as there are few paints that will adhere to wax.

Another method of aging paint is to rub it with waterproof sand paper. Faster than rubbing with steel wool, this is probably the most subtle of our aging techniques. It will leave the paint surface looking gently aged as well as wonderfully smooth. Use only the finest grades of paper, and always use them with plenty of water.

The following recipes are for a panel approximately 43ft.^{2} (4m.^{2}).

INGREDIENTS   **See swatch captions.**

EQUIPMENT   **3 containers / 2 x 4in. (100mm.) paintbrushes / 1 x 2in. (50mm.) paintbrush / tape measure / straightedge / water-soluble marker or chalk line / fine-grit sand paper / large bowl of water / cellulose sponge**

INSTRUCTIONS   **1** Prepare the surface thoroughly. See pages 26–9.

2 Mix each color in a container as you need it.

3 Use the two larger paintbrushes to apply two coats each of the base and top color, allowing each coat to dry thoroughly (2–4 hours).

4 Decide on the position and dimensions of your stripe. Ours is 8in. (20cm.) wide, and 8in. (20cm.) from the top of the panel. Measure and mark it out using the tape measure, straightedge, and marker (see page 39).

5 Use the smaller brush to paint in the stripe. Allow the paint to dry overnight.

6 Dip a postcard-sized piece of sand paper in water and use it to begin to rub away at the paneling. As you work, the

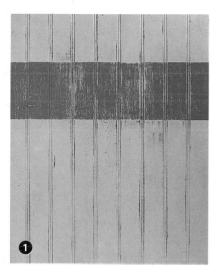

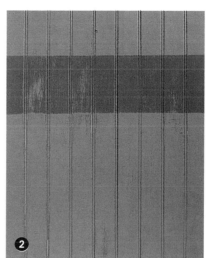

❶ OCHRE ON BUTTERMILK OVER BLACK Base coat: 17oz. (500ml.) black latex flat; top coat: 10oz. (300ml.) white latex flat, 6¾oz. (200ml.) yellow ocher, 10tsp. cadmium yellow. Stripe: 4oz. (120ml.) yellow ocher.

❷ GRAY ON GRAY GREEN OVER DUSKY PINK Base coat: 15oz. (450ml.) white latex flat, 4tsp. each Mars red and neutral gray. Top coat: 12oz. (350ml.) white latex flat, 4oz. (120ml.) neutral gray. Stripe: 4oz. (120ml.) neutral gray.

paint will come off in a slurry, and the piece of sand paper will start to get clogged up. Mop up the slurry with the sponge, rinse the paper out, and continue with the rubbing until you are happy with the effect. The paint will rub off more quickly on corners and edges.

MELTED-WAX RESIST

This technique exploits the incompatibility of wax and water-based paint to mimic old, peeling paint. For the best results, look at examples of genuine peeling paint to get an idea of how to apply your wax. The following recipes are for a panel approximately 43ft.^{2} (4m.^{2}).

INGREDIENTS See swatch captions (over).

EQUIPMENT 3 containers / 2 x 4in. (100mm.) paintbrushes / 1 x 2in. (50mm.) paintbrush / small glass jar / old saucepan / plate warmer (optional) / old artists' fitch / tape measure / straightedge / water-soluble marker or chalk line / spatula / fine-grit sand paper or fine steel wool

INSTRUCTIONS
1 Prepare the surface thoroughly. See pages 26–9.
2 Mix each color as you need it in a container.
3 Using one of the larger paintbrushes, apply two coats of the base color. Allow each coat to dry (2–4 hours).
4 Put the wax in the jar and the jar in a saucepan of boiling water. The wax will melt with the heat from the water. You can keep the water hot by using a plate warmer. Alternatively, replace the water from time to time with freshly boiled water. Do not attempt to melt the wax over a

AGING PAINT

❷ PEACH ON STEEL OVER FLAME
Here the base coat is simply 17oz. (500ml.) ready-mixed pimento red latex flat paint, and the top coat is 17oz. (500ml.) of another ready-mixed latex flat in cadet blue. The stripe uses 4oz. (120ml.) white latex flat combined with 1tsp. each Mars red and neutral gray. The resist is as for swatch 1.

❶ EAU DE NIL ON JADE OVER GREEN
This base coat uses 17oz. (500ml.) ready-mixed emerald green latex flat paint, with a top coat of 13½oz. (400ml.) white latex flat, 4oz. (120ml.) raw umber, 2tsp. phthalocyanine blue, and 4tsp. Payne's gray. The stripe is 5oz. (150ml.) white latex flat, mixed with 2tsp. cobalt blue and 1tsp. yellow ocher. The resist is 3–6tbsp. beeswax.

flame, as there is a danger that it will ignite.

5 Using the artists' fitch, apply the melted wax loosely but thickly to the paneling in random shapes. These will become the areas where the paint will appear to have peeled off.

6 Once the wax is hard, use a large brush to apply two coats of the top color, allowing 2–4 hours for each coat to dry.

7 Measure and mark out the 8in. (20cm.)-wide stripe.

8 Apply further drops of wax within the stripe, mostly over and around the wax that is already there.

9 Once the wax has hardened, use the smaller paintbrush to paint the stripe. Allow to dry (1 hour).

10 Next, use the spatula to scrape off the wax. You will easily be able to locate its thick layers beneath the paint. Of course, as you remove the wax, you will also take the paint with it, and this is what gives the aged effect.

11 You can now use either a piece of sand paper or steel wool dipped in beeswax to gently rub the whole paint surface back a little, smoothing off the sharp, new edges of paint left by the removal of the wax.

WHITING RESIST

Whiting mixed with water is a type of paint without a binder. When dry, it can easily be scraped off with a spatula, and it is water-soluble. Like wax, it can be used as a resist for an aged effect. It does not produce such refined results, but it has other advantages. One is that you can wipe it off easily at any stage, so if you do not like what you have done, you can simply and cleanly remove it. Second, because the whiting is water-based, it does not leave an oily or waxy residue. This means you can continue adding more coats of paint or glazes (see pages 179–81). The following recipes cover approximately 43ft.² (4m.²).

INGREDIENTS   See swatch captions.

EQUIPMENT   3 containers / screw-top jar / 2 x 4in. (100mm.) paintbrushes / 1 x 2in. (50mm.) paintbrush / artists' fitch / tape measure / straightedge / water-soluble marker / spatula / sponge / fine-grit sand paper or fine steel wool / 2tbsp. beeswax

INSTRUCTIONS   **1–3** Follow the instructions for wax resist.

4 To make the resist, put the whiting, water, and wallpaper paste in the screw-top jar. Put the lid on and shake vigorously for 30 seconds, then let the mixture stand for 5 minutes. If you find the mixture too thick or too thin—it should be thick and creamy—you can adjust the consistency by adding either water or whiting as appropriate.

5 Using the fitch, apply the resist in random blobs and shapes. As with the wax resist, these will become the areas where the paint will appear to have peeled off. Leave to dry for 1–2 hours.

6 Next, use another of the larger paintbrushes to apply two coats of the top color, allowing 2–4 hours for each coat to dry completely.

7 Measure and mark out the 8in. (20cm.)-wide stripe.

8 Use the fitch to apply more blobs of resist to the stripe, mainly over and around the resist that is already there.

9 Once the resist has hardened off—about 1–2 hours—use the smaller paintbrush to paint the stripe in the stripe color. Allow to dry (1 hour).

10 Now use the spatula to carefully scrape off the resist and the paint layers with it. When you have finished, you will see that a residue of whiting is left on the surface. Wash this off with a wet sponge.

11 Finish as for the wax resist.

❶ **SLATE ON BLUE OVER LILAC** This base coat is 15oz. (450ml.) white latex flat mixed with 1tbsp. neutral gray and 1tsp. dioxazine purple. The resist is 10tbsp. whiting, 5tbsp. water, and 1tsp. wallpaper paste. The top coat is 17oz. (500ml.) ready-mixed medium-blue latex flat, while the stripe is in 5tbsp. Payne's gray, 1tbsp. white, 2tsp. burnt umber, and 1tbsp. phthalo-cyanine green.

❷ **SALMON ON EAU DE NIL OVER GREEN** The base coat is 17oz. (500ml.) ready-mixed latex flat paint in light sea-green, and the top coat is 15oz. (450ml.) white latex flat mixed with 2tbsp. cobalt blue and 1tbsp. yellow ocher. The resist is as for swatch 1. The stripe is in 5oz. (150ml.) white latex flat mixed with 2tbsp. naphthol red and 4tsp. cadmium yellow.

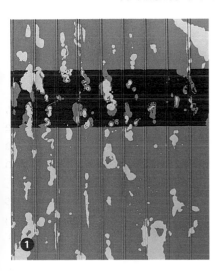

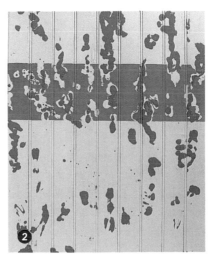

STIPPLING

This technique, used to stipple the blocks of color on pages 111–13, is another way to achieve a soft finish, but, unlike colorwashing or dry brushing, the brush marks disappear, to be replaced with a misty, slightly grainy texture. Normally stippling is carried out with oil-based paints, which give you more time to work up the texture before the paint dries. But, as we show here, it is possible to stipple using water-based paints, provided the area you tackle is kept small. We did not use a special brush to do the stippling. They do a good job but are expensive. When working on this scale, you can achieve perfectly acceptable results with a large, fat paintbrush, and it is easier to stipple into the corners.

Our diamond motif—formed by masking with torn masking tape—has been repeated to make a border, but it could be applied singly or in small groups to decorate door panels or a table top.

The following recipes are for approximately 54ft.^{2} (5m.^{2}).

STIPPLED DIAMONDS

INGREDIENTS   **See swatch captions.**

EQUIPMENT   **2 containers / paint roller plus tray / tape measure / carpenter's level / water-soluble marker / masking tape / 1 x 3in. (75mm.) paintbrush / large paintbrush for stippling / sponge**

INSTRUCTIONS   **1** Prepare the surface thoroughly. See pages 26–9.
2 Mix the background color in one of the containers and apply two coats using the roller, allowing 2–4 hours for each coat to dry.
3 Plan the position of your border, and mark it out lightly using the tape measure, carpenter's level, and the marker. The height of each of our diamonds is 8in. (20cm.) and the width is 6in. (15cm.).
4 Tear the masking tape along its length, and use to mask out alternate diamonds (see pages 34–5).
5 Mix the stipple glaze in the other container, and apply this in a thin layer to one of the masked-out diamonds using the large paintbrush.
6 Immediately take up the other clean, dry brush, and begin to dab it all over the surface of the wet glaze. Keep up the dabbing action until all the brush marks have disappeared and are replaced with an even, allover, grainy texture. Work quickly—once the paint starts to dry, you will no longer be able to continue with the stippling.
7 Repeat the same process for each of the masked-out diamonds in turn.

❶ RUST ON LILAC
Here, the background color is 12oz. (360ml.) white latex flat, mixed with 2tbsp. magenta and 1tbsp. Payne's gray. The diamonds are stippled using 1tbsp. Mars red mixed with 5oz. (150ml.) acrylic glazing liquid and water in the ratio 1 part color : 10 parts glazing liquid : 3 parts water.

❷ EGGPLANT ON PISTACHIO
This background color is 13½oz. (400ml.) white latex flat, mixed with 10tsp. yellow ocher, 2tsp. black, and 1tsp. phthalocyanine green. The glaze is 1tsp. dioxazine purple, 1tsp. white, and ½tsp. raw sienna mixed with 4oz.(125ml.) acrylic glazing liquid and water in the ratio 1 part color : 10 parts glazing liquid : 3 parts water.

❸ CHARTREUSE ON MIDNIGHT
Against this background color of 7½oz. (220ml.) white latex flat, mixed with 7½oz. (220ml.) black latex flat and 4tbsp. phthalocyanine blue, are diamonds stippled in 1½tsp. cadmium yellow medium, ¾tsp. white, and ¾tsp. raw umber, mixed with 5oz. (150ml.) acrylic glazing liquid and water in the ratio 1 part color : 10 parts glazing liquid : 3 parts water.

8 Remove all the masking and leave to dry for at least 2 hours before masking out the remaining diamonds. Stipple these in the same manner.

9 Remove the masking from the final set of diamonds and allow to dry (2–4 hours). Clean off any marker from the wall with a damp sponge.

COMBING

This involves dragging a purpose-made comb through wet paint to leave a pattern of ridges similar to the look of a woven fabric. The combs are usually sold in sets, giving a choice of three different-sized teeth in four or five widths of comb. You can achieve similar effects with tile-cement spreaders or with homemade combs cut from plastic or cardboard. These recipes will cover approximately 43ft.² (4m.²).

COMBING OVER COLORWASHING

INGREDIENTS
See swatch captions.

EQUIPMENT
Choose from the following:
Screw-top jars / paint roller plus tray / small paint bucket / 1 x 4in. (100mm.) paintbrush / safe-release masking tape / cash register tape / 3–4in. (75–100mm.)–wide broad-toothed comb / rag / sand paper

INSTRUCTIONS

1 Prepare the surface thoroughly. See pages 26–9.

2 Mix the first color—the background and combing color— in a screw-top jar. Using the roller, paint on two coats, allowing 2–4 hours for each coat to dry.

3 Mix the colorwash in another screw-top jar and use the two larger brushes to apply two coats (see pages 44–5), allowing 2 hours between coats and overnight for the second coat to dry.

4 Using masking tape for delicate surfaces in conjunction with cash register tape, mask out the border (see pages 34–5). If the border is going to turn a corner, as here, miter the corner also with masking tape.

5 Using the smaller brush, apply a liberal amount of the first color along a 3–6ft. (1–2 m.) section of the border. Don't skimp. It must be thick enough for the comb to leave it standing up in ridges.

6 Without hesitation, drag the comb across the wet paint at

❶ WISTERIA OVER PEA GREEN
Here the first color is 17oz. (500ml.) white latex flat mixed with 1tbsp. ultramarine. The colorwash is 2tbsp. white latex flat, 4tbsp. cadmium yellow and 2tsp. raw umber, mixed with 3½oz. (100ml.) acrylic glazing liquid and 13½oz. (400ml.) water.

❷ LINEN OVER HYACINTH
The first color is 17oz. (500ml.) white latex flat with 5tsp. raw umber. The colorwash is 4tbsp. white latex flat, and 2tsp. each ultramarine and dioxazine purple, mixed with 5½tbsp. glazing liquid and 11oz. (320ml.) water.

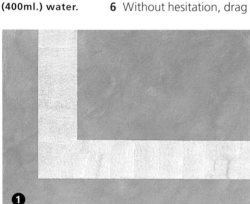

❶

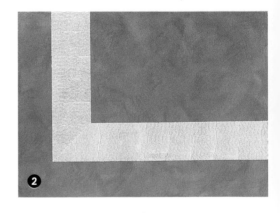

❷

right angles to the masking tape. Do not stop until you reach the opposite edge of the border. As you pull the comb across, vary the pattern by increasing and decreasing the pressure on it or by allowing it to wander in gentle wavy lines. Reposition the comb in the adjacent area of wet paint, slightly overlapping the first, and pull it across the paint once more. You will occasionally need to wipe excess paint from the comb with a damp rag.

7 Repeat along the border until you reach the corner, as it is not easy to join wet combing to dry. Remove any masking tape and leave to dry thoroughly. As the paint is rather thick, this may take longer than the normal recommended drying time of 4 hours.

8 Mask the other sides of the miters, and repeat the combing on the remaining sides.

9 Remove the masking along the edges of the border to reveal a crisply edged border with a ribbed finish.

COMBING UNDER COLORWASHING

This makes the combed band more subtle. It is carried out in exactly the same manner as described above, except that the combing is done first and the colorwashing second. After colorwashing, sand the combed ridges very lightly with sand paper dipped in water.

❶ WISTERIA UNDER DANDELION YELLOW
The background and combing color are 17oz. (500ml.) white latex flat mixed with 1tbsp. ultramarine. The colorwash is 4tbsp. white latex flat, 4tsp. yellow ocher, and 2tsp. each phthalocyanine green and Payne's gray, mixed with 6tbsp. acrylic glazing liquid and 12oz. (360ml.) water.

❷ LINEN UNDER CLEMATIS
The background and combing color are once again 17oz. (500ml.) white latex flat mixed with 5tsp. raw umber, as in swatch 2 of combing over colorwashing, while the colorwash consists of 2tbsp. each dioxazine purple, quin-acridone red, and white latex flat, mixed with 6tbsp. glazing liquid and 9oz. (270ml.) water.

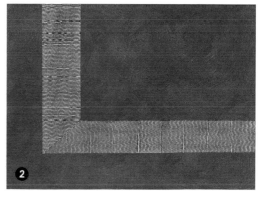

STUCCO & EMBOSSING

Acrylic modeling pastes come in a variety of textures and can be colored with acrylic paint. We particularly like those with a very fine, sandy texture like stucco. They can be spread into a stencil with a palette knife, or can take a stamped impression. We use both techniques here. The wave is such a simple shape that, if you want to use it as a border, you can cut it as one long stencil from cardboard or paper. To use it as a repeat pattern, begin by masking out the spacing for it along a line, then stencil alternate sections. The following recipes are sufficient for a 16ft. (5m.) long border of two wavy lines.

STENCILED WAVE WITH STUCCO STARFISH

INGREDIENTS

See swatch captions.

EQUIPMENT

Choose from the following:
Tracing paper / pencil / paper / repositionable spray adhesive / stencil board / X-Acto knife / cutting mat / large eraser or four small ones stuck together / container / paint roller plus tray / tape measure / string or chalk line / screw-top jar / cellulose sponge / ceramic tile / artists' palette knife

INSTRUCTIONS

❶ BLUE STUCCO STARFISH
The background is 17oz. (500ml.) light bronze latex flat, the wave 4tbsp. cobalt blue and 4tsp. white, while 40–50 starfish need 3tbsp. modeling paste with ½tbsp. white and ¼tsp. phthalocyanine blue.

1 Prepare the surface thoroughly. See pages 26–9.
2 Trace the motifs on page 182, enlarge them on a photocopier, and use to make the wave and starfish stencils (see pages 30–31).
3 Mix the background color, and use the roller to apply two coats, allowing 2–4 hours for each coat to dry.
4 Measure and mark out the positions of the wave (see page 39), then mix the wave color. Spray the back of the wave stencil with adhesive, position it, and sponge in the color (see page 50). Remove the stencil, then stencil a second wave below it. Allow to dry (1 hour).
5 Mix the modeling paste and the starfish color together on a tile with the palette knife.

❷ YELLOW STUCCO STARFISH
The background is 17oz. (500ml.) white latex flat with 2tsp. Payne's gray and 4tsp. phthalocyanine green. The wave is as in swatch 1, while the starfish need 3tbsp. modeling paste with 2tsp. yellow ocher.

6 Spray the back of the starfish stencil with adhesive and place it on the wave. The positioning is random. Using the palette knife, spread a thin layer of the modeling paste into the stencil to a depth of $\frac{1}{16}$in. (1–2mm.). Aim to keep the mixture inside the stencil, allowing as little as possible on the face of the stencil. This will help you to maintain a clean edge to your starfish as you lift the stencil off the surface.

7 Very gently remove the stencil, place it in the next position, and repeat the process until the design is complete. Since the colored modeling paste is thicker than normal acrylic paint, it will take an hour or more to dry. After a day, it will be extremely hard and durable.

STUCCO WAVE WITH EMBOSSED STARFISH

INSTRUCTIONS

1–3 Follow the stenciled wave instructions, but this time make a wave stencil and, from an eraser, a starfish stamp (see page 32).

4 Mark out the positions of the wave . Use the palette knife to mix the modeling paste and wave color on a tile.

5 Spray the back of the wave stencil with adhesive, position it, and use the palette knife to pile the modeling paste onto the stencil to a thickness of about $\frac{1}{16}$in. (1–2mm.), as in step 6 of the stenciled wave.

6 The modeling paste is soft enough to take an impression, but we find it more successful to leave it for 5–6 minutes. As it is sticky, the stamp will adhere to it. That is why we use it with a powder pigment or, as here, with metallic powder. This not only prevents sticking—just as flour prevents dough from sticking to a rolling pin—but also leaves a colored impression. Tip the powder onto a piece of paper, press the stamp into it, then press the stamp into the still-damp paste.

7 Dip the stamp into the metallic powder for each subsequent impression. Leave a full day to harden off.

❶ EMBOSSED RED STARFISH The background is the same as for the blue stucco starfish. The wave needs 8½oz. (250ml.) acrylic modeling paste with 3tbsp. phthalocyanine blue artists' acrylic color, and the starfish is embossed with 2tbsp. Venetian red metallic powder.

❷ EMBOSSED GREEN STARFISH The background is as for the yellow stucco starfish, and the wave, although it does not appear so, is as for the embossed red starfish. This is due to simultaneous contrast between the blue and ocher of swatch 1, which makes the blue look lighter than it is. Here the starfish is embossed with 2tbsp. emerald green metallic powder.

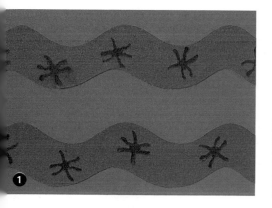

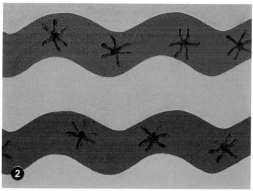

STONE FINISHES

Stone comes in many colors and textures, and reproducing it in paint can be complicated. Nevertheless a reasonable resemblance to some of the less exotic stones is possible. The main pieces of equipment you need are nothing more than a cellulose sponge and a bowl of water. These recipes will cover approximately 4m² (43ft²).

LIMESTONE, SANDSTONE, AND GRANITE

INGREDIENTS See swatch captions.

EQUIPMENT 3 or 4 containers / coarse-textured paint roller plus tray / 3 or 4 cellulose sponges / scissors / bowl of water / 2 x 3in. (75mm.) paintbrushes / masking tape / 1 or 2 spray bottles / denatured alcohol / large plate / short-haired fitch / stick

INSTRUCTIONS

❶ LIMESTONE
The joint color is 6tbsp. white latex flat and 2tsp. raw umber. For each of the following, begin with 6tbsp. white latex flat. For the base color, add ½tsp. each yellow ocher and raw umber. For the first glaze, 1tsp. raw umber and 2tsp. yellow ocher, and for the second, 2tsp. neutral gray and ½tsp. yellow ocher. Add dabs of yellow ocher, gray, and white.

1 Prepare the surface thoroughly. See pages 26–9. If you do not want joint lines, go straight to step 3. Otherwise, mix the joint color and brush it on in an uneven layer. Allow to dry completely (4 hours).

2 Using torn masking tape, mask out a pattern of ragged-edged joint lines over the painted surface.

3 Mix the base color and use the roller to apply one coat. Allow to dry (1 hour).

4 Trim two or three cellulose sponges (see pages 22–3).

5 Using the first glaze, follow steps 3–5 on page 52.

6 If you want a finer texture, reduce the amount of water and use a spray bottle to apply some of it. You can also work with a finer sponge.

7 A further variation is to splash or spray on denatured alcohol. The water and color will flow away from the denatured alcohol, forming yet new shapes.

8 For color variation, sponge on dabs of other suitable colors. Once you have achieved the desired effect, allow to dry (1–2 hours), then remove any masking tape.

❷ GRANITE
For the joints, mix 4tbsp. white and 2tbsp. black latex flat. The base coat is 6tbsp. white latex flat and 2tsp. neutral gray. The first glaze is 4tbsp. Payne's gray, 2tbsp. white, and 4tsp. burnt umber, while the second glaze is white. To finish, spatter on ¼tsp. each of black and white, softened with a spray of denatured alcohol.

❶

❷

9 Mix the second glaze and apply it in the same way as before, adding dabs of color if you wish. Leave to dry thoroughly.

10 For the finish of a stone such as granite, spatter on black and white paint. Load a short-haired fitch with diluted paint and tap it hard against a stick held 12–16in. (30–40cm.) from your work. A longhaired brush will spatter everything around. The consistency of the paint is important. Too thin and you will splash, not spatter; too thick and the paint will not leave your brush.

SLATE

INGREDIENTS   **See swatch captions.**

EQUIPMENT   **1 or 2 containers / cellulose sponge (optional) / masking tape (optional) / 1 x 3in. (75mm.) paintbrush / spatula / wax**

INSTRUCTIONS   **1** Follow steps 1 and 2 above, but sponge on the joint color instead of brushing it on.

2 Use the decorators' brush to apply one coat of the base color and allow to dry (4 hours).

3 Mix the slate color, and use the spatula to apply it in a not-too-thick layer to a small area. Smooth out the paint, using small circular movements. As it begins to dry, add a little wax and rub it in along with the paint. This burnishing action will give a hard, polished, slatelike finish. You will soon see when to add the wax, and will discover how to make slight changes to the patina by varying your timing.

4 While still working on the first area, you can start to spread and burnish fresh paint alongside. You can work on two or three areas at the same time. Work across the whole surface without stopping to prevent any joints from showing. Allow to dry for a day.

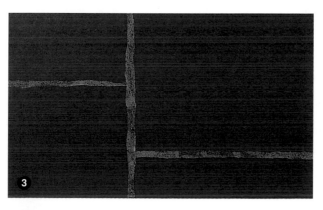

❸ SLATE
The joint color is the same medium-gray as for granite, while the slate base color is 3½oz. (100ml.) black latex flat. The slate color consists of 5tbsp. Payne's gray, 1tbsp. white, 1tbsp. phthalo-cyanine green, and 2tsp. burnt umber.

PAINTING ON GLASS

To judge by the tenacity with which splashes of paint cling to windows, one would imagine that you could decorate glass with almost any type of paint. But special glass paints—opaque for signwriting, transparent for stained-glass effects, and frosting varnish for an etched-glass look—are available. It is these last two that we have used for the designs here.

You can apply the paint either with a brush or a sponge. It is very liquid, so any masking must be really well stuck down to prevent the paint from seeping behind. Once the painting is complete, found objects such as leaves or postage stamps can be stuck between this sheet and a second one, the two held together with binder clips.

The recipes will decorate a sheet of glass 12in.² (30cm.²).

PAINTED GLASS FRAMES

INGREDIENTS   **See swatch captions.**

EQUIPMENT   **Ruler / pencil / paper / 2 sheets of glass, 12in.² (30cm.²) / masking tape / small piece of cellulose sponge, its corners trimmed off / saucer / small, round artists' brush / solvent for glass paint / 4 binder clips with removable wire levers**

INSTRUCTIONS   **1** Prepare the surface thoroughly. See pages 26–9.
2 Draw a 12in. (30cm.) square on a sheet of paper and within this square rule a tic-tac-toe grid of four lines at 4in. (10cm.) intervals. Rule a further four lines, ⅜in. (10mm.) out from the first.
3 Copy the motif on page 182. Either trace it onto or glue photocopies of it in the center of each of the corners of the grid you have drawn.
4 Attach the drawing to the back of one of the pieces of glass and hold it in place with tape at the center of each edge. Place the glass face up on a level surface.
5 Tear masking tape along its length, and stick it firmly on the glass along the first set of grid lines, leaving the four corners exposed.
6 Pour a little of the first color onto a saucer, and use a small piece of cellulose sponge to apply it to each of the corners. You must paint the color on all at once. Any attempts to apply a second coat will only result in the first coat being disturbed or removed. Leave to harden off (1 hour), then remove the masking tape.
7 Using the artists' brush and the second color, paint in lines of dots at approximately ⅜in. (1cm.) intervals along the second set of lines. Fully load the brush and just dab it onto

❶ GOLDEN OLIVE CORNERS
All the colors are ready-mixed glass paints. The first color is olive green, the second violet, and the third, turquoise.

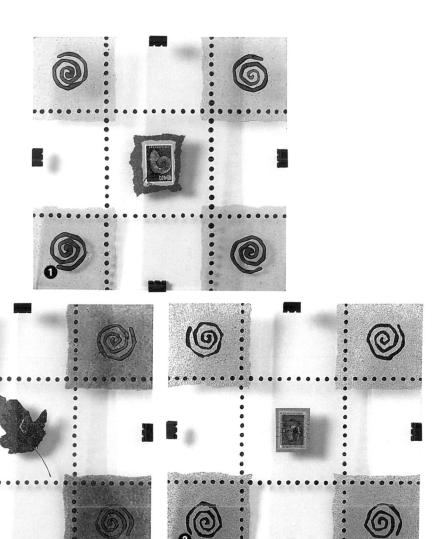

❷ SLATE GRAY CORNERS
Again, the colors are ready-mixed glass paints. The first is gray, the second magenta, and the third, golden brown.

the surface to make the dot. Allow to dry (2 hours). As soon as you have completed the dots, clean the brush in solvent; otherwise, the paint will harden in the bristles and the brush will be of no further use.

8 With the artists' brush and the third color, paint in each of the spirals. Again, fully load the brush and let the paint flow off it as you follow the line of the design seen through the glass. Allow to dry (2 hours). Immediately clean the brush with solvent as before.

9 You can now assemble the frame but as the paint will not be fully cured for a number of days, you should handle it with care. We have used the frames to trap small decorative items—postage stamps and leaves in these examples. These have been stuck in place on the second piece of glass. Hold the two pieces of glass together with the binder clips, then remove their levers.

❸ BRONZE METALLIC CORNERS
Here the first color is 1oz. (30ml.) frosting varnish mixed with a scant ¼tsp. bronze powder, and the second and third colors are both gray glass paint.

STENCILING

Stencils are common decorators' devices. They are partly a way of controlling where your paint goes and partly a way of making repeat patterns. In these examples we have endeavored to keep our stencils simple. This makes them easy to cut and also gives them a more modern look, which we prefer.

When stenciling, use repositionable spray adhesive, both to hold the stencil in place as you work and to stop paint from seeping under its edges. Spray the back of the stencil lightly, protecting the surrounding surfaces with newspaper. The spray is highly toxic, so always spray in a well-ventilated area and avoid breathing it.

The following recipes are for approximately 17oz. (500ml.) of background color and 7–8tbsp. of stencil color—enough, probably, for an average wall. We have applied all our backgrounds with a roller.

INGREDIENTS

See swatch captions.

EQUIPMENT

Choose from the following:
Large container / large paint roller plus tray / tracing paper / pencil / paper / stencil board / repositionable spray adhesive / cutting mat / X-Acto knife / scissors / tape measure / ruler / compass / carpenter's level / water-soluble marker / string / scraps of cardboard / masking tape / screw-top jars / saucers / sponges

SIMPLE STENCILING

Perhaps the most commonly used design for a simple stencil is the *fleur-de-lis*, a favorite motif of interior decorators and now a classic. Lettering has an equally long history as a decorative motif but also allows you an element of personalization. You could stencil your initials across a wall, floor, window, or any other surface. The stencil is easy to cut and use, but a disciplined layout is essential for a classy look.

INSTRUCTIONS

1 Prepare the surface thoroughly. See pages 26–9.
2 Trace the motifs from an alphabet in a lettering book or from an old manuscript. Plan the layout and the size of your stencil in unison. Our motif is 7 x 4in. (18 x 10cm.), cut from a piece of stencil board 12 x 8in. (30 x 20cm.). To assist in top-to-bottom positioning, rule light lines 3in. (8cm.) below the required positions of the letters using a level and water-soluble marker (use string on large areas). Then cut the stencil motif with its lowest part 3in. (8cm.) up from the lower edge of the stencil board. By placing this edge of the stencil board on your marked line each time you stencil, you will always be assured of a correct position.
3 Spray the back of the stencil with adhesive, and, starting

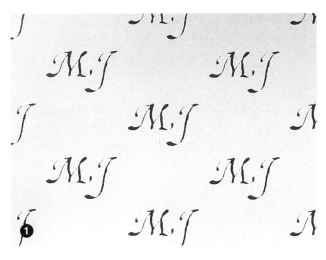

1 GRAY-BLUE BACKGROUND AND DEEP MAGENTA
For this background, mix 10tsp. cobalt blue and 10tsp. Payne's gray into 17oz. (500ml.) white latex flat. For the stencil color—a surprisingly intense contrast against the background—add 4tsp. white and 2tsp. yellow ocher to 3½oz. (100ml.) magenta.

from the left, place it in its first position on one of the lines. Sponge in the color and remove the stencil.

4 Use a spacing bar to determine side-to-side placements. This is a scrap of cardboard attached to the side of the stencil with masking tape. Attach the spacing bar to the left of the stencil. Reposition your stencil to the right for the second print, aligning the left-hand end of the bar with the right-hand edge of the first motif. If you want a 10in. (25cm.) space between motifs, the left-hand end of the bar should be 10in. (25cm.) from the left edge of the cutout motif in the stencil. Sponge in as before.

To stencil to the left of your first image, you will have to attach the spacing bar to the right-hand edge of the stencil.

5 Repeat along the marked lines until you have completed your design. Note how, in our example, each stenciled image is set half a space along from the one above.

OVERLAPPING STENCILS

Simple stencils can be designed to link up to create flowing borders. Here, a tendril and a flower have been stenciled together along a line.

INSTRUCTIONS

1 Prepare the surface thoroughly. See pages 26–9.

2 Trace each motif on page 182 separately, together with their registration holes. Enlarge them on a photcopier and use to make the stencils (see page 30). The registration holes should be carefully positioned on each stencil.

3 Rule a line along the wall at the height you would like your border, and place one of the stencils on it with its holes over the line. Lightly mark the wall through the registration holes, using a water-soluble marker.

STENCILING

❶ PALE YELLOW BACKGROUND WITH FUCHSIA PINK
The background is 1tbsp. each Hansa yellow light and raw umber with 18½oz. (550ml.) white latex flat. The tendrils are in 4tbsp. white, 2tbsp. raw umber, 1½tbsp. Payne's gray, and 1tbsp. phthalocyanine green. The flower is 3½oz. (100ml.) magenta with 4tsp. white and 2tsp. yellow ocher.

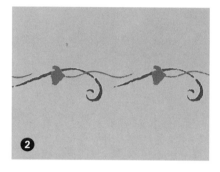

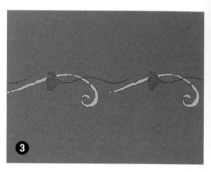

❷ LABURNUM BACKGROUND WITH BLUE GRAY
The background is 17oz. (500ml.) laburnum yellow latex flat with tendrils in 3½oz. (100ml.) magenta with 5tsp. burnt sienna. The flowers are 6tbsp. white and 1tbsp. Payne's gray.

4 Move the stencil along the line toward the right until the right-hand mark shows through the stencil's left-hand hole. Mark the wall again through the right-hand hole. Continue in this way until you have set all the registration marks along the ruled line.

5 Beginning with the tendril, lightly spray the back of the stencil and place it in its first position, lining it up so that its holes are over the first two marks. Sponge in the color.

6 Move the tendril stencil to the position after next, and sponge this in the same way, and so on along the line. By the time you reach the end, the first stenciled tendrils will have dried enough for you to stencil those in between.

7 The flower stencil is sponged in over the top of the tendril, using exactly the same registration marks.

❸ BRONZE BACKGROUND WITH BLUE
The base coat is 17oz. (500ml.) light bronze latex flat with tendrils in 6tbsp. white, 2tbsp. Hansa yellow light, and ¼tsp. raw umber. The flowers are 4tbsp. white, 4tbsp. cobalt blue, and 1tsp. dioxazine purple.

SHADED STENCILING

A second color sponged over the first can give a simple, flat stencil a three-dimensional look. These shaded circles and squares have soft edges, as their stencils have been torn into shape rather than cut.

INSTRUCTIONS

1 Prepare the surface thoroughly. See pages 26–9.

2 To make the stencils, draw a 2in. (5cm.)-diameter circle and a 4in. (10cm.) square on separate pieces of stencil board. Begin by making a hole in the center of each board, then delicately tear out the shapes as close as possible to the line.

3 Tear two strips of cardboard, each about 6 x 1½ in. (15 x 4cm.), down their long edge.

4 Plan the spacing of your motifs, and use a washable marker to mark out the surface to be decorated. The squares here are spaced at 4in. (10cm.) intervals and the circles at 2in. (5cm.) When positioning the motifs, use either the notches or the spacing bar method (see page 69).

5 To stencil a circle, attach the circle stencil with spray adhesive, and sponge quite densely using the first color. With the stencil still in place, take a sponge sparsely loaded with the second color and dab it on, starting on one side of the circle and gradually moving inward. Aim to create a gentle gradation of tone that follows the form of the circle, transforming it into a ball.

6 For a square, place the stencil in position and lightly sponge in the first color. With the stencil still in place, position one of the strips of cardboard across the diagonal, leaving the lower, triangular half of the square exposed. Sponge this in densely with the same color.

7 Reposition the strip across the other diagonal, leaving the opposite lower half exposed, and sponge this in lightly with the second color.

8 Place the second strip across the first, leaving a small triangle exposed on the bottom edge of the square. Sponge this in densely with the second color. Remove all the strips of cardboard to reveal a pyramid with each face in a different color made up of the various layers and densities of paint.

❶ JORDAN ALMOND BACKGROUND
The background is 17oz. (500ml.) palest dusty pink latex flat, and the first stencil color is 4tbsp. white, 2tbsp. cobalt blue, and 1tbsp. yellow ocher. The second requires 6tbsp. Hansa yellow light, 2tbsp. white, 2tsp. yellow ocher, and ½tsp. raw umber.

❷ SHELL PINK BACKGROUND
This background is 17oz. (500ml.) light shell pink latex flat, and the first color is 6tbsp. white, 1tbsp. ultramarine, 2tbsp. dioxazine purple, and 1¼tsp. black. The second color is 4tbsp. white, 4tbsp. Mars red, and 2tbsp. cadmium yellow medium.

❸ HEATHER GRAY BACKGROUND
The background is 17oz. (500ml.) heather gray latex flat and the blue is 6tbsp. ultramarine, 3tbsp. white, and 1½tsp. quin-acridone violet. The acid yellow uses a mixture of 4tbsp. white, 4tsp. Hansa yellow light, and ¼tsp. raw umber.

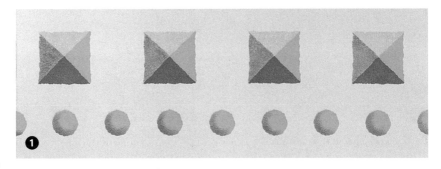

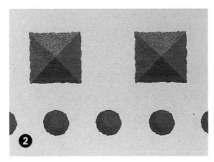

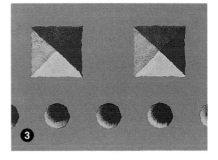

STAMPING

Like stencils, rubber stamps are an effective way of reproducing a motif, but they are much quicker to use, producing a soft, varied texture which suits both contemporary and more traditional interiors. You can buy ready–made rubber stamps, but it is not difficult to make your own (see page 32). Acrylic paint is ideal for stamping. If the stamp is small, press it onto a layer of paint rolled out on a tile. For larger stamps, apply the paint to the stamp with the roller (see page 33).

Practice stamping on a scrap of paper to discover how much paint you need and how much pressure to apply. The following recipes will cover approximately 43ft.[2] (4m.[2]).

INGREDIENTS   **See swatch captions.**

EQUIPMENT   *Choose from the following:*
Container / paint roller plus tray / tape measure / water-soluble marker / string / cardboard (optional) / 6 x 10in. (15 x 25cm.) foam-rubber mat / 6 x 10in. (15 x 25cm.) foamcore backing board / clear paper cement / 2 screw-top jars / 2 ceramic tiles / small paint roller / bowl of water / 1 or 2 sponges / ordinary marker / tracing paper / pencil / paper / X-Acto knife

A SIMPLE STAMP

This design uses one square stamp twice to produce a motif with a shadow of itself behind. It could be stamped at random but, as with the stenciling (see pages 68–9), we prefer a more orderly arrangement.

INSTRUCTIONS   **1** Prepare the surface thoroughly (see pages 26–9) and use the roller to paint on two coats of background color, allowing 2–4 hours for each coat to dry.
2 Measure and mark out the layout, using string as a guide for each of the horizontal lines of squares.
3 Mark out the spacing between each square with the water-soluble marker, or cut a piece of cardboard to the width of the space required and use this as a guide.
4 Make a 1½in. (4cm.)-square stamp of foam rubber, glued

❶ PALE SHADOWS
The background is 6¾oz. (200ml.) white latex flat mixed with 10oz. (300ml.) yellow ocher. The first stamp color is ¼tsp. Payne's gray with 1¾oz. (50ml.) white latex flat, and the second is 1¾oz. (50ml.) Payne's gray. These will each print approximately 100 squares.

to a backing board of the same dimensions (see page 32).

5 Mix the two colors, and spoon some of the first onto a tile. Roll out a generous, even layer and press your stamp into it. Stamp lines of squares along and up the wall. Clean the stamp by patting it up and down in a little water or on a wet sponge, then gently dry it with a cloth.

6 Press the stamp into a little of the second color on a tile. The second motif overlaps the first, a little below and to the left of it. To get it in the right place each time, mark a line on the upper and right-hand edges of the backing board, and align these with the left-hand side and lower edge of the first squares each time you print.

AN ORNATE STAMP

This stamp is in two sections, but there is no reason why any number of sections should not be used, depending on your patience and ingenuity. It has been designed to make a border, but it could be used for an allover pattern.

INSTRUCTIONS

1 Follow the instructions for simple stamping.

2 Measure for the lower edge of the border, and tightly stretch a string along this line.

3 Trace the motif on page 182, enlarge it to 8½in. (22cm.), and cut out the two sections. Arrange them on the foam rubber and use as templates (see page 32). The stamp will print as a mirror image, so its two sections must be the right way around. Draw a line on the reverse of the backing board opposite the tip of the motif to help with lining up.

4 Mix the stamping color and spoon some onto a tile. Roll it out with a small roller, then roller over the stamp to deposit an even film of paint on it. Place it in position, lining up its bottom edge with the string, then press firmly.

5 Repeat to complete the border. Because there is no spacing between motifs, when you print, you must place the end of the stamp alongside the end of the previous motif.

2 PAYNE'S GRAY ON PALE OCHER This background is the same as that used for the simple stamp, and the stamp color is again ¾oz. (50ml.) Payne's gray, but this amount will print only 50 of these larger motifs.

2

6 You may come up against an obstruction such as a window, door, or corner where you will not be able to stamp a complete motif. If the empty spaces are very small and unobtrusive, you can simply leave them as they are. If you have finished the rest of your border and have only one or two more spaces to fill, you can cut the stamp down to make a motif that will fit the spaces. This will be easy to do if you have used a foamcore backing board. If you need a lot more motifs, stamp several prints on paper, and cut them out to make paper stencils which you use only once. Bend the paper stencils into corners or cut them to fit up to doors or windows, then sponge on the paint, mimicking the texture of the design as a whole.

A TWO-STAMP DESIGN

Here we employ the already prepared simple stamp and ornate stamp to make a third, more elaborate design, which we use as a border.

INSTRUCTIONS

1 Follow the instructions for simple stamping.

2 Use a tape measure to measure out two lines spaced 8½in. (22cm.) apart. Tightly stretch strings along these lines.

3 Follow step 5 of a simple stamp, printing the squares at 4in. (10cm.) intervals inside the two lines. Note how the squares of the lower line are staggered to the right by the width of one square.

4 Spoon a little of the second color onto a tile, roll it out, and roll it over the second stamp. Print this vertically between the squares, using the string and the squares as a guide. Make sure that the top and bottom points of the second stamp fall exactly between two squares. You should not need any complex marking out, provided you have cut the backing board of the second stamp square and its stamp is centered on it.

❸ PALE GRAY AND PAYNE'S GRAY
Again, the background color is the same as that already used, and the first and second stamp colors are as before.

The principle of resists is quite simple. Apply a design in a resist to a background, then paint over it and the surrounding area. The resist will prevent this layer of paint from adhering. Once it is dry, remove the resist together with the paint, to reveal the design in the background color. The following recipes will cover approximately 43ft.^{2} (4m.^{2}).

PAINTED-WAX RESIST

INGREDIENTS   **See swatch captions.**

EQUIPMENT   **2 containers / 2 x 3in. (75mm.) paintbrushes / tracing paper / pencil / paper / chalk / jar or can / saucepan / plate warmer (optional) / small artists' fitch or other small artists' brush / spatula / sand paper (optional)**

INSTRUCTIONS   **1** Prepare the surface thoroughly (see pages 26–9) and use a paintbrush to give it two generous layers of background color, allowing each coat 2–4 hours to dry.
2 Trace the heart on page 182, enlarge it on a photocopier, and trace it onto the surface.
3 To melt the wax, place a tablespoon in a jar in a pan of freshly boiled water. As it cools, you may have to replenish the water or keep it hot on an electric plate warmer. Never heat the wax over direct heat, as it is highly flammable.
4 Use an artists' fitch to paint the wax into the design. It will harden almost immediately. Do not use your favorite brush, as it will be useless for water-based paint afterward.
5 Mix the topcoat and brush it on. Leave an hour or so to become touch-dry, then use a spatula to remove the wax, leaving the motif in the background color.
6 To give an aged effect around the heart, sand the top coat slightly with sand paper dipped in water.

❶ **LEMON UNDER SAGE**
The background is a mixture of 5tbsp. white latex flat with 8tsp. Hansa yellow light, and the top coat is 4tbsp. white latex flat mixed with 1tbsp. neutral gray and 1¼tsp. phthalocyanine green. The resist is 1tbsp. soft wax.

❷ **CERULEAN UNDER EGGPLANT**
This background is a mixture of 6tbsp. white latex flat with 2tbsp. phthalocyanine blue, and the top coat is 2tbsp. neutral gray, 4tsp. raw umber, and 2tsp. dioxazine purple. The resist is the same as for swatch 1.

RESISTS

SPRAY-WAX RESIST

Using aerosol beeswax polish in conjunction with a stencil is easier for decorating large areas than using a painted-wax resist.

INGREDIENTS   **See swatch captions.**

EQUIPMENT   **Paint roller plus tray / stencil board / pencil / X-Acto knife / cutting mat / tape measure / water-soluble marker / repositionable spray adhesive / paper / aerosol beeswax polish (see page 20) / paper towels / container / 2 x 3in. (75mm.) paintbrushes / rags / mineral spirits**

INSTRUCTIONS

1 Prepare the surface thoroughly (see pages 26–9), and use a roller to give it two coats of background color.

2 Cut the simple motif below from stencil board and measure and mark out its positions on the wall.

3 Attach the stencil to the wall with spray adhesive, then protect the surroundings with paper. Spray the wax evenly into the stencil. Remove the stencil and blot excess wax from it using paper towels. To prevent wax from getting on the back of the stencil while you do this, lay it flat on a smooth surface such as a Formica-topped table or sheet of glass.

4 Carefully replace the stencil in the position after next, spray with wax as before, then repeat for all alternate positions. Allow the wax 2–3 hours to harden, then, if some is still wet, blot it up by pressing gently, not rubbing, with paper towels. Stencil the remaining sections.

5 Mix the colorwash, paint this over the wax resist (see pages 44–5), and allow to dry (15–20 minutes).

6 Soak a rag in mineral spirits and rub the design very firmly to break through the paint and dissolve the wax below, leaving a slightly tinted broken-edged design.

❶ BRONZE
The background is 1qt. (1 liter) white latex flat, and the topcoat is 9oz. (270ml.) ready-mixed pumpkin latex flat, diluted in the ratio 4 parts water : 1 part color.

❷ DUSKY BLUE
Here the background is 1qt. (1 liter.) white latex flat, and the topcoat is 8½oz. (250ml.) white latex flat, mixed with 2tsp. black and 2tsp. phthalocyanine blue, diluted as for swatch 1.

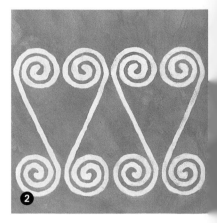

WHITING RESIST

A resist made from whiting, water, and a pinch of wallpaper paste is a cheap and solvent-free alternative to wax, although it does not give quite such a refined finish. It makes a water-soluble paint which can be washed off very easily and leaves no residue. This means that you can wipe it off at any time during the procedure and also paint on more layers of paint or glazes, since no waxy residue will have been left.

INGREDIENTS **See swatch captions.**

EQUIPMENT **Paint roller plus tray / paper / 1 small and 1 medium artists' brushes / pencil / screw-top jar / container / 1 x 4in. (100mm.) paintbrush / spatula**

INSTRUCTIONS

1 Prepare the surface thoroughly (see pages 26–9), and use a roller to give it two coats of background color.

2 Use one of the artists' brushes to paint a flick of a freehand oval on paper, enlarge it on a photocopier, and trace it carefully onto the wall.

3 Combine all the resist ingredients in the jar, put the lid on securely, shake hard for 30 seconds, then let stand for 5 minutes. The resist should be thick and creamy. If it is too thin, add a little whiting; if too thick, add more water.

4 Using the two artists' brushes, fill the motif with a thick layer of resist, following the outline as accurately as you can. Leave to dry for an hour or more.

5 Mix the topcoat and use a soft paintbrush to paint on two coats. The resist will crumble easily, so do not be too robust. Allow each coat to dry (2–4 hours).

6 With a spatula, gently scrape away the resist and its covering of paint. It will come off in a powder which can be swept away and any residue washed off.

❶ SALMON
The background is 1qt. (1 liter) white latex flat, with a topcoat of 10oz. (300ml.) white latex flat, mixed with 5oz. (150ml.) raw sienna and 5tsp. magenta. The resist is 10tbsp. whiting, 5tbsp. water, and 1tsp. wallpaper paste.

❷ BARLEY
Here the background is again 1qt. (1 liter) white latex flat, with a topcoat of 13½oz. (400ml.) white latex flat, mixed with 3½oz. (100ml.) yellow ocher. The resist is as in swatch 1.

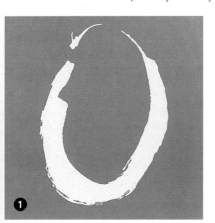

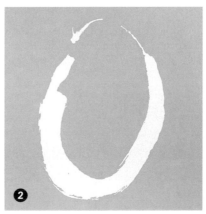

MASKING

Masking tape or paper masking can be used to build a design. Tapes vary in size and stickiness. Whichever you use, be sure not to take the paint off when you remove the tape. For larger areas we make masking papers cut or torn into shape and sprayed with repositionable adhesive. Do not use newspaper, as the ink will be dissolved by the adhesive and transferred to your surface. The backs of old photocopies are very suitable or, as in our torn-paper cross, cash register tape torn along its length. These recipes will cover approximately 43ft.^{2} (4m.^{2}).

BROKEN COLUMN BORDER

INGREDIENTS
See swatch captions.

EQUIPMENT
Container / paint roller plus tray / tape measure / chalk line / ¾in. (20mm.) safe-release masking tape / ¾in. (20mm.) masking tape for straight lines / ¾in. (20mm.) masking tape for curves / tracing paper / pencil / paper / screw-top jar / saucer / sponge

INSTRUCTIONS
1 Prepare the surface thoroughly. See pages 26–9.
2 Mix the background color in the container, and use the roller to apply two coats, allowing 2 hours between coats. Leave overnight to dry.
3 Decide on the position and scale of your design. Mark it out on the wall using the tape measure and chalk line, and mask off the top and bottom edges of the border with the masking tape for delicate surfaces. Trace the column motif on page 182, enlarge it on a photocopier, and trace it between the two lines of tape, positioning it at a different angle for each motif.
4 Mask out each element of the design using the appropriate masking tape for straight lines and for curves or

❷ **SIENNA AND SMOKY BLUE**
The background is a mix of 14oz. (420ml.) white latex flat, with 5tbsp. Payne's gray. The sponged color is 4½oz. (125ml.) white latex flat, and 4½oz. (125ml.) raw sienna.

❶ **VENETIAN RED AND CREAM**
Here the background is 17oz. (500ml.) white latex flat tinted with 5tsp. raw umber. Sponged over it is a mixture of 3½oz. (100ml.) vermilion, 10tsp. magenta, 10tsp. white, and 4tsp. dioxazine purple.

❶

❷

create a paper mask.

5 Mix the second color in the screw-top jar, spoon some onto a saucer, and use a sponge to apply it loosely to the border. To achieve an uneven, textured effect, do not press too hard.

6 Slowly and carefully peel off the masking tape to reveal the design. Leave to dry.

TORN-PAPER CROSS

INGREDIENTS See swatch captions.

EQUIPMENT 2 containers / standard paint roller plus tray / smooth paint roller plus tray / tape measure / water-soluble marker / masking tape / cash register tape / repositionable spray adhesive

INSTRUCTIONS

1 Prepare the surface thoroughly. See pages 26–9.

2 Mix the background color in a container, and use the standard roller to apply two coats, allowing 2 hours between coats and overnight to dry.

3 Decide on the position and size of your cross. It could be one big cross, or several smaller ones. Use a tape measure plus water-soluble marker or bits of masking tape to measure and mark its outer limits and approximate center. Tear cash register tape along its length, and attach it to the wall to form the cross, using the spray adhesive.

4 Mix the second color in a container, and use the smooth roller to apply two coats. Do not lean too hard on the roller, as the paper mask, once it is wet, is likely to wrinkle, and paint will be forced below it.

5 Remove the masking and allow to dry (2–4 hours).

❶ PEA GREEN OVER SOUR CREAM
The background to our cross is 17oz. (500ml.) white latex flat, 2tsp. cadmium yellow, 2tsp. yellow ocher, and 1tsp. neutral gray. Over it is 10oz. (300ml.) white latex flat, with 3½oz. (100ml.) yellow ocher, 10tsp. phthalocyanine green, and 10tsp. Payne's gray.

❷ SLATE OVER STONE
Begin with a mixture of 17oz. (500ml.) white latex flat and 1¾oz. (50ml.) raw umber. Over this, apply a second coat of 8½oz. (250ml.) white latex flat, 8½oz. (250ml.) Payne's gray, and 2tbsp. phthalocyanine green.

PART THREE

PROJECTS & DESIGNS

An inspiring array of ideas for decorating every surface in the home—walls, floors, doors, windows, furniture, and accessories—each in a choice of colors to show what can be achieved.

To paint this seedhead frieze (see pages 96–9), we used a large stencil in a rather unusual way. Instead of stenciling on paint, as you might expect, we filled the stencil area with sprayed-on beeswax resist, then followed it with paint. For a smaller design you could apply ordinary wax with a spatula.

WALLS

The story of wall painting is as old as painting itself. However, we would not attempt to draw any comparisons between the cave art of 17,000 years ago, and what we propose you can do to your back bedroom, except to say that the techniques and pigments used are not all that different. Cave paintings also testify to the durability of water-based paints and to the powers of attraction of a blank wall to someone with a can of paint in one hand and a paintbrush in the other.

The desire to enrich or embellish walls with color, pattern, motifs, or symbols has been present in most cultures, even if in the past the embellishment was mostly confined to the walls of ceremonial or religious buildings, or to the homes of the rich. Wall decoration now has more to do with style, aesthetics, and good design than with symbolism, even if today's motifs and colors have been borrowed from Romanesque churches or Greek temples.

The art of painting designs on walls fell into decline in many parts of the world with the introduction of wallpaper. Paint, if it was applied at all, was in one flat color. But now, the desire for the precision of a wallpaper pattern which unrolls down a wall regardless of architectural features, is perhaps being replaced by a wish for something more personal and handcrafted. Part Two of this book showed what can be achieved using simple techniques. Here, in Part Three, those ideas have been developed further, with stencils, stamps, and masks used on walls, often in conjunction with colorwashing or sponging to create designs ranging from

Above: With its asymmetry and large scale, this single-hue scheme is reminiscent of certain contemporary American paintings. The color theme continues through the furnishings and across the floor.

Left: A stenciled wall decoration by Charles Rennie Mackintosh for The Hill House in Dumbartonshire, Scotland. A design from the beginning of the century, but it is still fresh today.

simple borders to allover patterns.

Borders have many uses. They can be shrunk to fit the smallest of places—but avoid being over-fussy—or they can grow to the size of a frieze. They can soften the division between painted areas, or between ceiling and wall. Alternatively, they can provide a decorative band across a plain wall. You can also use a border to make frames or panels on large walls or chimneys. None of this thinking is new, of course. Borders used in these ways go back as far as the ancient world, where some fine examples have been found in archaelogical sites such as Pompeii and in Egyptian tombs.

Left: This border, painted with loose flicks of a brush above a rudimentary colorwash, adds charm to an old rough wall.

Below: Bands of color are ever-popular and ever-useful. Here, enlivened by a scattering of flowers, they appear to sink into the plastered wall.

Allover patterns are the other alternative for walls. But by allover, we do not necessarily mean that you cover every wall in a room. Concentrated and busy designs are often better if they are confined to a single wall, a counter front, or an alcove, especially if the room is intended to be a place of relaxation. You will also doubtless need some wall space to hang pictures, so you should aim to strike a balance between using applied designs and using the more subtle techniques of sponging or colorwashing.

You could, of course, adapt many of the designs in this part of the book for use on other surfaces, but by and large, we designed them for walls. But, don't be afraid to experiment, both with color combinations and designs, using your wall as a place to test your ideas and see how they look full size. After all, a wall is the easiest surface to recoat with latex when you have finished. But the one piece of advice we would offer is not to apply more than one design to a room at any one time. Your decoration should be noticeable, but do not let it overwhelm either the room, or you.

STRIPED GREEK VASES
IN AN ALCOVE

This big design is contained within an alcove, bringing some life to a part of the home that usually has shelving. As you can see, it will even cohabit happily with the shelving. Drawing the design is made easy with the use of a single template, cut down for each successive vase. Each part of the design is masked out in turn, taking particular care when going around curves.

BASIC RECIPE—MEDITERRANEAN

PREPARATION

Prepare the surface thoroughly. See pages 26–9.

INGREDIENTS

Background ▶ 17oz. (500ml.) pale gold latex flat paint
Rectangle ▶ First wash: 3½oz. (100ml.) white latex flat paint / 3½oz. (100ml.) water; second wash: 4tbsp. cobalt blue artists' acrylic color / 4tsp. white latex flat paint / 2¾oz. (80ml.) water
Vases ▶ First color: 3½oz. (100ml.) white artists' acrylic color / 1¾oz. (50ml.) water; second color: 2¾oz. (80ml.) white latex flat paint / 4tsp. Mars red artists' acrylic color / 1¾oz. (50ml.) water; third color: 2¾oz. (80ml.) white latex flat paint / 4tsp. yellow ocher artists' acrylic color / 1¾oz. (50ml.) water; fourth color: 4tbsp. cobalt blue artists' acrylic color / 2tbsp. white latex flat paint / 3tbsp.water
Stripes and shading ▶ 4tbsp. white artists' acrylic color

EQUIPMENT

Medium-textured paint roller plus tray / tape measure / straightedge / carpenter's level / water-soluble marker / safe-release masking tape / flexible masking tape or Fineline tape (see page 36) and masking tape / cash register tape / 6 large, deep plates / 4 x 4in. (100mm.) paintbrushes / 13ft. (4m.) lining paper / string / pencil / scissors / several pieces of soft cloth / sponge

INSTRUCTIONS
Background

Use the roller to apply two coats of the background color, allowing 2–4 hours to dry between coats.

Rectangle

1 Mark out a 4 x 5ft. (1.2 x 1.5m.) rectangle. Mask it off with masking tape and cash register tape (see pages 34–5).
2 Mix the washes for the rectangle. You can mix enough for each on a deep plate unless you happen to need a lot, in which case use a paint bucket. Apply two coats of each wash to the rectangle, using the paintbrushes (see pages 44–5), allowing 1 hour for each coat to dry. Leave overnight after the final coat. Remove the tape from the top and right-hand edges of the rectangle.

STRIPED GREEK VASES IN AN ALCOVE

Vases

1 Prepare the template of the large vase (see page 187). Place it in position, so that it overlaps the left-hand side of the rectangle and extends about 6in. (15cm.) below it.

2 Draw around the template with the water-soluble crayon, then mask around this line using the appropriate masking tape (see page 36).

3 Mix the first vase color in a deep plate, then roll a small piece of cloth into a pad, dip it into the paint, and rub it into the right-hand side of the vase, where it overlaps the rectangle. Use a variety of movements to create a random texture. Allow to dry (1 hour).

4 Repeat a second and third time using a fresh pad of cloth each time. The first coat may look a little irregular, but by the time you have finished the third, you will have evened out any raggedness. Leave to dry thoroughly overnight without removing the masking.

5 Meanwhile, cut the template down to make the medium vase by removing an 8in. (20cm) band from its center and trimming the rim along the lines shown (see page 187). Join the two halves with masking tape.

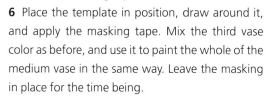

6 Place the template in position, draw around it, and apply the masking tape. Mix the third vase color as before, and use it to paint the whole of the medium vase in the same way. Leave the masking in place for the time being.

7 Returning to the large vase, remove the masking from the bottom and left-hand edges of the rectangle, but leave the tape around the vase. Mask off the section of the vase that is still to be painted.

8 Rub three layers of paint into this section of the vase exactly as before, using the cloth and the second vase color.

9 Cut the template down a second time by removing another 8in. (20cm.) band from its center and trimming the base and rim as shown (see page 187). Join the two new halves together with masking tape.

10 Remove the masking tape from the left-hand edge of the large vase, and position the new template so that it overlaps the large vase, forming an ellipse. Draw around the template and mask its edges with masking tape. Mask off the ellipse by positioning a piece of masking tape on its inside edge.

11 Using the same technique as before, rub three layers of the fourth vase color into the rest of the small vase.

12 Remove the masking tape from the inside edge of the

❶ PALE STONY GRAYS AND BLUES
In this variant, the base coat is made from 18oz. (540ml.) white latex flat with 8tsp. raw umber and 2tsp. Payne's gray. The first rectangle color is 3½oz. (100ml.) white latex flat, and the second is 5oz. (150ml.) white with 1tbsp. Payne's gray, both diluted with an equal amount of water. The first vase color is 3½oz. (100ml.) white latex flat with ½tsp. raw umber. The second is 3½oz. (100ml.) white latex flat with ½tsp. neutral gray and ¼tsp. cadmium yellow. The third is the base coat pale gray. The fourth vase color is the same as the second rectangle color. All four vase colors are diluted in the ratio 2 parts color : 1 part water. The stripes and shading use the first vase color.

ellipse, and reposition it on the outer edge where you have just painted the small vase. Rub three layers of the first vase color into the ellipse. Remove the masking tape and reposition it on the inside edge.

13 Mask out 4¾in. (12cm.)-wide horizontal stripes on the left half of the medium vase. Sponge these in the stripe color, aiming for a thick, slightly textured layer.

14 Mask out stripes 2½in. (6cm.) wide across the left-hand side of the small vase. Sponge these in the stripe color. Remove the masking from the inside edge of the ellipse, and reposition it on the outer edge, leaving the ellipse clear.

15 Mask out stripes 2½in. (6cm.) wide across the ellipse, being sure to alternate them with the stripes on the small vase, as in the example. Sponge in the stripe color.

16 Finally, use the stripe color to sponge in shading along the right-hand edge of the large vase. The masking tape will still be in place along this edge, but you will need to define the lower edge of the rim with a fresh piece of tape. Remove all masking tape, and allow to dry thoroughly.

❷ GRAYED PINKS, BROWNS, YELLOWS, AND GREENS
The background and third vase color is 20oz. (600ml.) white latex flat with 10tsp. burnt sienna. For the rectangle and fourth vase color, we added 4tsp. neutral gray, 3tsp. yellow ocher, and 1tsp. cadmium yellow to 4tbsp. white latex flat. The first vase color and the stripes are made from 6tbsp. white latex flat, 3tbsp. raw umber, and 1tsp. phthalocyanine green. The second vase color contains 3tbsp. raw umber, 1tbsp. burnt sienna, and 2tbsp. white latex flat. All four vase colors are diluted as in swatch 1. The colorwash needs 1 part color : 1 part water. The stripes and shading use the first vase color.

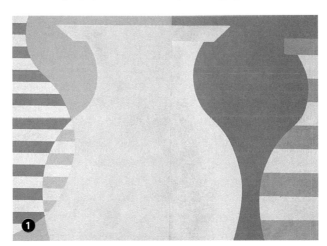

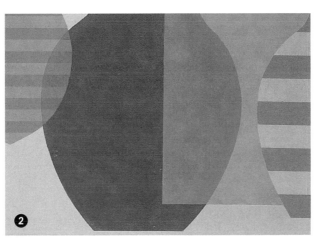

CHECKERBOARD
WALL

Don't let anyone persuade you that papering a wall is quicker and easier than stamping a design on it. Even if it were true, papering will never match the pleasure to be had from making your own stamp and using it across a wall. The end result will always have a quality that cannot be matched by any wallpaper. It will never be as perfect as, or have the complexity of, a wallpaper pattern, but if that is what you like, the chances are that you are reading this book by accident.

This simple stamp needs few registration marks. Once you have drawn the horizontals and a vertical on your wall, you can proceed, stopping only to change to the smaller stamps to negotiate awkward corners, electric outlets, and such.

BASIC RECIPE—STRAW ON OPAL

PREPARATION

Prepare the surface thoroughly. See pages 26–9.

INGREDIENTS

For a wall up to 43ft.² (4m.²)
Base coats ▸ 20oz. (600ml.) white latex flat paint / 1tbsp. cobalt blue artists' acrylic color / 2tbsp. yellow ocher artists' acrylic color / 2tbsp. Payne's gray artists' acrylic color
Motif ▸ 7½oz. (225ml.) white latex flat paint / 1tbsp. Hansa yellow light artists' acrylic color / 1tbsp. raw umber artists' acrylic color
Optional protective coat ▸ 10oz. (300ml.) matt acrylic varnish

EQUIPMENT

2 large containers / 1 large paint roller plus tray / 1 x 2in. (50mm.) paintbrush / plumb line / carpenter's level / water-soluble marker / 8 x 8in. (20 x 20cm.) foam-rubber mat / scissors or X-Acto knife / cutting mat / foamcore backing board / small tube clear paper cement / small paint roller / paper / masking tape / 1 x 2in. (50mm.) varnish brush (optional)

CHECKERBOARD WALL

INSTRUCTIONS

Base coats

1 Mix the color for the base coat in one of the containers, and stir well.

2 Apply two even coats to the wall with the large roller. Use the paintbrush to apply paint around any fixtures and into corners. Allow 4 hours for each coat to dry.

Design

1 Plan the layout of the pattern on the wall (see page 39), using the plumb line to set a vertical guide and the carpenter's level and a water-soluble marker to mark the horizontals.

2 Use the foam-rubber mat to make three stamps: one with four stripes, 6 x 6in. (15 x 15cm.), one with one stripe, 6 x ¾in. (15 x 2.1cm.), and one with half a stripe, 3 x ¾in. (75 x 2.1cm.). Attach them to backing boards of foamcore with clear paper cement (see page 32).

3 Mix the motif color in the other container and stir well. Apply paint to the square stamp, using the small paint roller (see page 33).

4 Following the vertical guide, stamp a line of motifs on your wall, reapplying paint to the stamp for each motif. Turn the stamp through 90° for alternate motifs in order to create the checkerboard effect. Repeat until most of the wall is covered. The square stamp will cover large areas of wall, but as you come up against corners or fixtures such as light switches, you will need to use the smaller stamps to complete the design, perhaps in conjunction with paper to mask off areas you have already completed.

Notes To prevent the paint from drying on your stamps if you decide to take a break while you are working, you should first gently clean them by dabbing them up and down in a bowl of water, then pat them dry on paper towels.

If your wall is likely to be knocked, kicked, or scuffed, use the varnish brush to give it a coat of varnish for protection.

❶ STRAW ON OPAL
The basic recipe.

❷ OPAL ON STRAW
Here the emphasis has been subtly shifted by reversing the basic color combination, printing the blue onto the yellow. Not only does the balance between the colors alter, making the blue more dominant, but the texture also shifts to the blue.

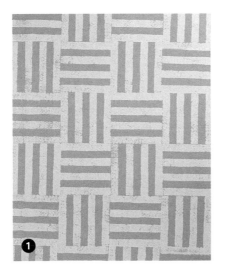

❸ STONE ON BRICK RED
These are the more robust colors of building materials—stone and red bricks. The strong contrast will make a splash in any room, so may need to be confined to a small area, or used to animate a dead corner. The red consists of 10oz. (300ml.) ready-mixed pimento red latex flat, mixed with 5tbsp. burnt sienna and 8tsp. white. The stone color is made from 10oz. (300ml.) white latex flat colored with 1tbsp. raw umber.

❹ WHITE ON STONE
This combination results in far less contrast. Pale colors such as these are more suited to large areas. while the subdued pattern will not clash with pictures on the wall. The base color is the stone used in swatch 3, overprinted with white latex flat. Couldn't be much simpler than that.

STAMPED SQUIGGLES
ON STRIPES

Stripes in any size will always be part of the interior decorators' repertoire. Without the stamped motif, these stripes would look good in either a formal setting or a very modern one, and many of you may want to leave it at that. But the addition of the stamp, which is easy to apply, makes the stripes more whimsical. The finished design, helped by its coloring, recalls French interiors from the past, but the dry brushing brings it more up to date. For an unregimented effect, choose stripes in random widths. These also have the advantage of being capable of adaptation to any length of wall. Here the randomness has been organized a little. All the stripes are in widths that are multiples of 2 inches (5 centimeters), and the colors have been applied in an ordered sequence, so it does look as if some thought has gone into the wall. The effect is restrained but lively.

BASIC RECIPE—RASPBERRY, DUSKY PURPLE, AND SALMON

PREPARATION
Prepare the surface thoroughly. See pages 26–9.

INGREDIENTS
For a wall up to 43ft.^{2} (4m.^{2})
Base coat ▶ 10oz. (300ml.) white latex flat paint
Stripe (i) ▶ 5tsp. magenta artists' acrylic color / 4tsp. white artists' acrylic color / 1tsp. raw umber artists' acrylic color / 10tsp. acrylic glazing liquid / water in the ratio 1 part water : 1 part glazing liquid : 1 part color
Stripe (ii) ▶ 5tsp. white artists' acrylic color / 2tsp. Payne's gray artists' acrylic color / ½tsp. dioxazine purple artists' acrylic color / 2½tbsp. acrylic glazing liquid / water in the ratio 1 part water : 1 part glazing liquid : 1 part color
Stripe (iii) ▶ 1½tbsp. white artists' acrylic color / 1½tbsp. magenta artists' acrylic color / 1tbsp. raw sienna artists' acrylic color / 1tbsp. dioxazine purple artists' acrylic color / 5tbsp. acrylic glazing liquid / water in the ratio 1 part water : 1 part glazing liquid : 1 part color
Motifs ▶ 1tsp. white artists' acrylic color / ½tsp. raw umber artists' acrylic color

EQUIPMENT
1 x 8in. (200mm.) medium-textured paint roller plus tray / tape measure / plumb line or carpenter's level / water-soluble marker / masking tape / 4 screw-top jars / 3 x 4in. (100mm.) paintbrushes / 4 ceramic tiles / tracing paper / pencil / paper / foam-rubber mat / scissors or X-Acto knife / cutting mat / foamcore backing board / small tube clear paper cement / small paint roller

STAMPED SQUIGGLES ON STRIPES

INSTRUCTIONS
Base coats

Use the medium roller to paint the wall with one or two coats of matt white latex flat paint. This should leave it opaque white with a slight orange-peel texture. Allow 4 hours to dry between coats, and at least 24 hours before the next stage.

Stripes

1 Divide the wall into stripes 6in. (15cm.), 8in. (20cm.), l0in. (25cm.), 12in. (30cm.), 14in. (35cm.), and 18in. (45cm.) wide. These should be arranged randomly, using the plumb line to ensure they are vertical (see page 39). You should mark the wall with the water-soluble marker. Mask out every third stripe.

2 Mix each of the three stripe colors in a screw-top jar. Apply color (i) to the masked-off stripes with a paintbrush, using the dry-brush technique (see pages 46–7). Allow to dry (2–4 hours), then remove the mask.

3 When color (i) is completely dry, mask off the next set of stripes, and apply color (ii) to them in the same way.

4 Finally, mask out the last set of stripes, and apply color (iii) to the wall using the same dry-brush technique.

Stamps

1 Trace the designs on page 182, enlarge them on a photocopier, and use them to make the two stamps (see pages 32-3). Our designs began life as tendrils, but metamorphosed into squiggles as the work progressed. Using clear paper cement, glue each stamp to a backing board that is ½in. (1.5cm.) longer than the stamp at each end. This will automatically give you the spacing between each print. Mark a center line on the side of the board that will face you as you print, and keep this aligned with the edge of the stripe as you proceed.

2 Mix the motif paint in the fourth screw-top jar, pour a little onto a tile, and apply it to one of the stamps with the small roller. Print the stamp down alternate lines where two stripes meet (see page 33). Turn the stamp through 180° for each alternate stamp.

3 Use the second stamp in exactly the same way down the other alternate lines.

4 You will not be able to use the stamps where the wall meets the baseboard or the ceiling. In order to continue the motif here, you will need to make some stencils. To do this, use the stamp to print the motifs several times on paper, then cut the paper to make stencils as required (see pages 30-31). These paper stencils can be re-used three or four times each.

❶ RASPBERRY, DUSKY PURPLE, AND SALMON
The basic recipe. If you find these colors too strong, modify them by adding water. Do not add more than two parts water, or the binder in the paint will be so diluted that the paint will not adhere to the wall.

❷ STRAW, HAY, AND CREAM
The yellows here consist of (i) 8tsp. white with ¼tsp. each Hansa yellow light and raw umber, and with acrylic glazing liquid and water in the same ratio as in the basic recipe; (ii) 4tsp. white mixed with 2tsp. Hansa yellow light, 1tsp. each yellow ocher and raw umber, and with acrylic glazing liquid and water as before; and (iii) 10tsp. white with 1tsp. each Hansa yellow light and raw umber, and ½tsp. yellow ocher, and with acrylic glazing liquid and water as before. This very subtle and soft set of colors is set off with a motif in color (ii) from the basic recipe.

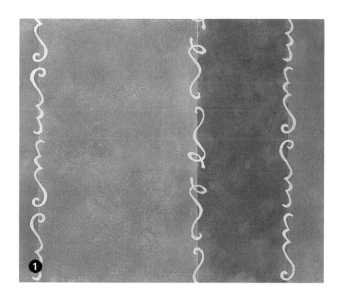

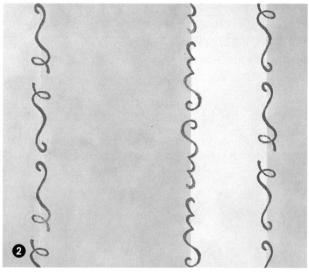

❸ FRENCH GRAY, DARK AND LIGHT JADE
For those who prefer the look of blues and gray, try (i) 10tsp. white mixed with 1½tsp. Payne's gray, ½tsp. each cobalt blue and yellow ocher, and with acrylic glazing liquid and water as before; (ii) 10tsp. white mixed with 2tsp. cobalt blue and 1tsp. yellow ocher, and with acrylic glazing liquid and water as before; and (iii) 6tsp. each of white and cobalt blue mixed with 1½tsp. yellow ocher, and with acrylic glazing liquid and water as before. For the motif, use off-white—10tsp. white tinted with ¼tsp. raw umber.

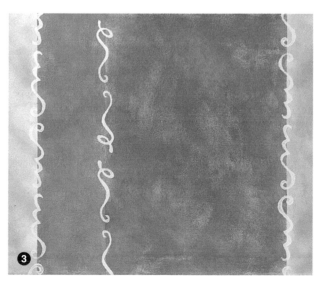

LATE-SUMMER SEEDHEAD FRIEZE

For many of us, this design is reminiscent of the autumn nature collections we made as children and displayed in jars in the school art room. There may be fewer wildflowers around now, but the memory of them can become a permanent installation, thanks to this delicate frieze of painted seedheads.

BASIC RECIPE—GOLDEN HAY

PREPARATION

Prepare the surface thoroughly. (See pages 26–9.) Apply two coats of paint to the wall in a color that will complement the frieze.

INGREDIENTS

To cover approximately 43ft.² (4m.²)
Base coat ▸ 17oz. (500ml.) thick, white, non-drip latex flat paint
Resist ▸ aerosol beeswax polish (see page 20)
Colorwash and shadows ▸ 10tsp. Hansa yellow light artists' acrylic color / 1tsp. raw umber artists' acrylic color
Protective coat ▸ 8½oz. (250ml.) clear polish or beeswax

EQUIPMENT

Paper / tape measure / repositionable spray adhesive / 2 x 4in. (100mm.) paintbrushes / plasterers' float / tracing paper / paper / X-Acto knife / stencil board / cutting mat / water-soluble marker / paper towels / screw-top jar / large container / saucer / cellulose sponge / soft rags / mineral spirits / lint-free cloth

INSTRUCTIONS
Base coat

1 Use torn paper to mask off the area above the frieze. This will create a soft, natural edge in keeping with the design. Do not be tempted to use old newspaper, as the spray adhesive may dissolve the ink and transfer yesterday's news onto your clean wall. Instead, use the clean side of old photocopies. Set the torn edge of the paper about 24in. (60cm.) up from the baseboard, and attach it to the wall with the spray adhesive.
2 Use a paintbrush to apply a thick layer of the latex flat to the wall beneath the paper, and spread it out using the plasterers' float. The aim is to create a patchy texture with vertical marks running up and down the design. Leave the paint to dry overnight.

Stencil

1 Trace the seedhead design (see page 183), enlarge it on a photocopier, and make it into a stencil (see page 30). Do not forget to cut the notches on the left of the stencil.
2 Set out the spacing for the design on the wall by

positioning the stencil at the left-hand side of the frieze. Use the water-soluble marker to mark the position of the right-hand side of the stencil on the baseboard and on the paper masking. Move the stencil along until its notches are lined up with these registration marks. Make two more marks where the right-hand edge of the stencil is now. Continue in this way along the wall.

Resist

1 Spray the back of the stencil with adhesive, and place it in its first position.

2 Cover the area all around with paper for protection, then spray the beeswax into the stencil (see page 76).

3 Remove the stencil from the wall and clean off excess wax from the front of the stencil using paper towels. To do this, lay the stencil down on a smooth surface—a Formica-topped kitchen table would be ideal—and dab the wax off, making sure that none goes on the back of the stencil.

4 Reposition the stencil in the position after next, using the marker registration marks and the notches as a guide. Spray with wax again. Continue along the wall in this way, cleaning up the stencil each time you use it, until you have completed every alternate position on your frieze. Leave to dry (2–3 hours). If there is any wax on the wall that is still wet at this point, blot it off carefully with paper towels, but do not rub it, or the wax will spread where you do not want it to go.

5 Repeat steps 1–4 on the remaining alternate sections.

Shadows

1 Mix the shadow color in the screw-top jar. Place half the mixture in the large container and put to one side.

2 Clean the stencil thoroughly, then reposition it on the wall half the width of the stencil to the right of its original position. Set out the registration marks in the new position.

3 Pour a little of the shadow color into a saucer, then lightly sponge and rub in the paint. Move the stencil along the wall as before and repeat the sponging. This will create the shadows of the seedheads that appear behind and to one side of the resist images. Allow to dry (30 minutes).

❷ DUSKY MAUVES
The colors in this swatch have been made from 2tbsp. white, 2tsp. dioxazine purple, 1tsp. ultramarine, and ½tsp. black applied as in the basic recipe over troweled-on white latex flat. This is a some-what more subdued solution for a subtler interior.

❶ GOLDEN HAY
The basic recipe gives a warm, sunny design that will brighten a room even when the sun is not shining.

❸ SAGE AND LEMON
Here, a wash of 10tsp. Hansa yellow light, diluted with water as in the basic recipe, was applied before the wax resist. The shadow color—also the base for a second wash is 10tsp. white, ¼tsp. phthalocyanine blue,1tbsp. raw umber, and ½tsp. Payne's gray.

Colorwash

1 Use the remaining shadow color to make a colorwash in the ratio 4 parts water :1 part paint. Use the two paintbrushes to colorwash the whole of the frieze (see pages 44–5), then leave to dry (15–20 minutes).

2 Soak a soft rag in mineral spirits and rub the motifs fairly firmly to remove the wax. As you do so, you will reveal the background color which the beeswax will have tinted a warm, amber white. Don't overdo the rubbing if, like us, you prefer to leave a little texture on your motifs.

Protective coat

To protect your work, you should wax it by applying polish with a lint-free cloth. Finally, remove all the masking, and you will have completed your field of seedheads casting their shadows on your wall.

SLOT-MACHINE
COUNTER FRONT

Generally, all-over designs on walls must not be too busy or they will dominate a room, but in many homes there are small areas that can be given more adventurous treatment. This design, inspired by a slot machine, was chosen partly because of the ease with which the motifs could be applied using large, simple stencils. We were quite playful with the design, but aimed for a degree of sophistication because of the counter's location in a dining area. Hence we rejected garish colors in favor of a more subdued palette. The effect was enhanced by sponging the colors on, leaving some of the background showing through.

BASIC RECIPE—MULTICOLORED

PREPARATION

Prepare the surface thoroughly. See pages 26–9.

INGREDIENTS

For a counter front up to 32ft.^{2} (3m.^{2})
Base coats ▶ 13½oz. (400ml.) white latex flat paint / 1tsp. each yellow ocher and cadmium yellow artists' acrylic color
Motifs ▶ (artists' acrylic colors used throughout)
Stripes ▶ 4 tbsp. white
Plums ▶ 2tbsp. white / 1tsp. dioxazine purple / 1tsp. ultramarine blue
Lemons ▶ 2tbsp. white / 4tsp. yellow ocher / 1tsp. cadmium yellow
Cherries and stars ▶ 1tbsp. white / 4tsp. yellow ocher / ½tsp. naphthol red
Lucky sevens ▶ 2tbsp. white / 2tsp. yellow ocher / 1tsp. phthalocyanine blue / 1tsp. Payne's gray
Bells ▶ 2tbsp. white / ¼tsp. black / ¼tsp. phthalocyanine blue

EQUIPMENT

1 x 8in. (200mm.) medium-textured roller plus paint tray / container / 7 saucers / 1 large and 6 smaller pieces cellulose sponge / tape measure / carpenter's level / water-soluble marker / masking tape / tracing paper / pencil / paper / stencil board / repositionable spray adhesive / X-Acto knife / cutting mat / string / 5 screw-top jars

SLOT-MACHINE COUNTER FRONT

INSTRUCTIONS

Base coats

1 Use the roller to apply half the white latex flat to the front of the counter. Allow to dry (2–4 hours).

2 Pour the remaining latex flat into the container, and add the yellow ocher and cadmium yellow. Stir well. Spoon some of this mixture into a saucer, and, using the large sponge, apply evenly to the counter front, leaving little flecks of the white base coat showing through (see page 50). Allow to dry (2–4 hours).

Layout

1 Divide the counter front into groups of three bands, as you would see on a slot machine. On our counter, the three 16½in. (42cm.) wide bands for the motifs are separated by 2in. (5cm.) wide white stripes. There is a 2¾in. (7cm.) wide white stripe at each end of both sets of three bands, and a 2in. (5cm.) wide gap at the center. Mark out all the lines with a water-soluble marker and use a carpenter's level to check that they are completely vertical.

2 Mask out for the white stripes (see pages 34-5). Spoon the white stripe color, a little at a time, into a saucer, and apply it using a small sponge.

Stencils

1 Cut your stencil board to the width of the widest bands. Trace the images on page 183, enlarge on a photocopier, and use to make the stencils (see page 30), making sure that the images are centered before cutting. Include the notches from the images. These will act as registration marks, enabling you to line up the stencils correctly.

2 The stenciled motifs are positioned along horizontal lines 12in. (30cm.) apart. To mark for these, stretch a piece of string from one side of the counter to the other, making sure it is the same distance from the floor at each end. Place masking tape at the points where the strings cross the white lines. Repeat for all the horizontal lines.

3 Lightly spray the back of the first fruit stencil with adhesive, and position it between the white lines, with its notches lined up with the masking-tape horizontals.

4 Mix each of the motif colors in a screw-top jar. Matching the paint to the stencil, spoon some of the color you are going to use into a saucer. With a small sponge, stencil the motif on as evenly as possible (see page 31), but allow the base coat to show through a little. Remove the stencil, then repeat using each of the other fruit stencils.

5 Repeat using the bells, lucky sevens, and stars stencils in the same way and with their respective paints.

6 To achieve the shadows on the fruits, reposition each stencil, then lightly sponge on the second color, taking care not to overload the sponge with paint. Beginning at the bottom edge of each fruit, dab the color on lightly. Keep your sponge on the move, and as it dries out, move it in toward the center so that the color fades out gradually. Reload your sponge as necessary, but take care not to overdo the shading or it will look too heavy. The plum is shaded using the blue of the bells, the cherries in the plum color, and the lemon with the cherry color.

7 The bells, lucky sevens, and stars do not have shadows. Instead, frame them, using the final stencil, which is, in fact, a half-frame. First position the stencil to make the upper half of the frame, and then the lower half. The sponging leaves no seams. The sevens are framed in the cherry red, the stars in the plum color, and the bells in the yellow of the lemons.

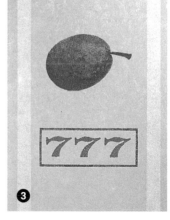

❶ CHERRIES AND BELLS
The cherries use a mixture of white, yellow ocher, and naphthol red, and are shaded with the plum color. The bells are sponged in a mixture of white, black, and phthalo-cyanine blue, and are framed in the lemon yellow.

❷ STARS AND LEMON
The lemon is sponged in a mixture of white, yellow ocher, and cadmium yellow, and is shaded with the cherry color. The stars use the cherry red and are framed in the plum color.

❸ PLUM AND SEVENS
The plum is made of white, dioxazine purple, and ultramarine blue, and is shaded with the blue of the bells. The lucky sevens are a mixture of yellow ocher, white, phthalocyanine blue, and Payne's gray, and are framed in the cherry red.

GUSTY STRIPES

This idea was inspired by a style popular during the reign of Gustavus III of Sweden (1771–92), but soon moved on. We wanted to mimic, in a stylized manner, the effect of peeling paint. The result has certain similarities to camouflage as well, especially in our choice of colors. These strong stripes pass over the shelves on our wall, and there is no reason why they could not continue over other fixtures too, for example, over doors or across window frames. They are perhaps best suited to a hall or entrance, or to a single wall or bay in a room.

BASIC RECIPE—ACHROMATIC STRIPES

PREPARATION **Prepare the surface thoroughly. See pages 26–9.**

INGREDIENTS *To cover 75–86ft.² (7–8m.²)*
Base coat ▶ 17oz. (500ml.) white latex flat paint / 2tbsp. black latex flat paint
First stripe ▶ 8½oz. (250ml.) black latex flat paint
Second stripe ▶ 4¼oz. (125ml.) white latex flat paint / 4¼oz. (125ml.) black latex flat paint
Resist paste ▶ 20tbsp. whiting / ½tsp. wallpaper paste / 10tbsp. water

EQUIPMENT **3 large containers / paint roller plus tray / 3 x 4in. (100mm.) paintbrushes / 1 x 1in. (25mm.) paintbrush / tape measure / plumb or chalk line / masking tape / screw-top jar / round fitch / scraper / sponge**

INSTRUCTIONS
Base color

Mix the base color in one of the containers. Apply this with a roller, and use brushes to get to places that the roller cannot reach. Leave to dry thoroughly, for at least a day.

1 Plan the layout of the stripes on the surface you are painting (see page 38). Our stripes are all 5in. (12cm.) wide. Mark their positions and mask off every other stripe using a tape measure, plumb line, and masking tape (see page 39).
2 Mix the first stripe color in another container and paint it on with the one of the larger brushes, finishing off the brush strokes in a vertical direction. Allow to dry (2 hours).
3 Meanwhile, mix the resist paste (see page 57) in the screw-top jar. As soon as the stripes are dry, you can use the fitch to dab, flick, and splotch the resist on in varying amounts. A resist made with whiting, as this one is, has many advantages over a wax resist, one of which is its ease of removal. This is an important factor if you are at all unsure of your design. Allow to dry (1 hour).

❶ ACHROMATIC STRIPES
The basic recipe.

❷ KHAKI GREEN STRIPES
Again a strong contrast is evident, but in a more natural color combination. The base coat of 17oz. (500ml.) white latex flat is colored with 1tsp. yellow ocher, ½tsp. phthalocyanine green, and ½tsp. black. The first stripe is 6¾oz. (200ml.) white latex flat with 5tsp. yellow ocher, ½ tsp. phthalocyanine green, and 1tsp. black. The darker top stripe starts with 8½oz. (250ml.) white latex flat mixed with 8tsp. black, 16tsp. yellow ocher, and 8tsp. phthalocyanine green.

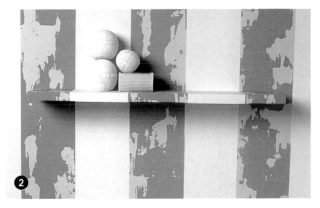

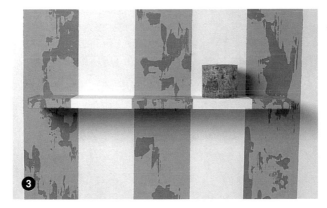

❸ KHAKI BROWN STRIPES
A softer choice. The base coat of 17oz. (500ml.) white latex flat has 4tbsp. raw umber mixed into it. The first stripe is 8½oz. (250ml.) ready-mixed very dark brown latex flat lightened with 4tbsp. white. The second stripe is a mix of 4oz. (125ml.) of the same latex flat and 4oz. (125ml.) white latex flat.

4 Mix the second stripe color in the third container, and use one of the larger brushes to apply it over the resist. The resist has wallpaper adhesive added to it to prevent the whiting from breaking up and ending up in smears in your paint. Nevertheless, apply the paint with care, or your resist will not live up to its name.

5 Allow this coat to set (1–2 hours), then remove the resist paste with a scraper, used delicately, and carefully clean off any residue using a damp sponge. Your final job is to very gently peel all of the masking tape from the wall to reveal the full effect of the dramatic stripes.

OAK-LEAF BORDER

Borders are a classic way of dividing up walls. They may be used at chair-height to divide a wall into an upper and a lower section or, as here, around a panel to create a frame. In this project, we have made an oak-leaf stamp from a piece of foam rubber, and used it to stamp a border marking the dividing line between an area of colorwashing and one of flat painting.

BASIC RECIPE—LINEN, RASPBERRY, AND SALMON

PREPARATION

Prepare the surface thoroughly. See pages 26–9.

INGREDIENTS

For a wall 43–54ft.^{2} (4–5m.^{2}) with a 26ft. (8m.) border
Colorwash ▶ 5tsp. naphthol red artists' acrylic color / 5tsp. white artists' acrylic color / 10tsp. acrylic glazing liquid / water in the ratio 1 part color : 1 part glazing liquid : 4 parts water
Flat paint ▶ 13½oz. (400ml.) white latex flat paint / 4oz. (120ml.) yellow ocher artists' acrylic color / 4tsp. Payne's gray artists' acrylic color
Leaf motif ▶ 1tbsp. white artists' acrylic color / 2tsp. Mars red artists' acrylic color

EQUIPMENT

Tape measure / chalk line and/or carpenter's level / water-soluble marker / 2 large containers / 2 x 5in. (120mm.) paintbrushes / safe-release masking tape / paint roller plus tray / tracing paper / pencil / foam-rubber mat / scissors or X-Acto knife / cutting mat / foamcore backing board / small tube clear paper cement / screw-top jar / ceramic tile / small paint roller

INSTRUCTIONS
Layout

Plan the layout of your design (see page 38), and mark the line between the colorwashed and the flat-painted areas using a water-soluble marker.

Background

1 Mix the colorwash in one of the large containers and brush it on (see pages 44–5), extending it to just beyond the marker line. Allow to dry thoroughly for at least 4 hours.
2 If the marker line is no longer visible, mark it out again, then mask off the colorwashed area with masking tape.
3 Mix the flat paint color and apply it using the roller. Apply a minimum of two coats in order to achieve an evenly flat matt surface, allowing 4 hours between coats. Remove the masking tape and allow to dry (4 hours).

Stamp

1 Meanwhile, trace the motif on page 184 and use it to make the stamp (see pages 32–3).
2 In our design the leaf is stamped at 2in. (5cm.) intervals

❶ LINEN, RASPBERRY, AND SALMON
The basic recipe.

❷ MIDNIGHT, ACID YELLOW, AND BLUE GRAY
Here the colorwash is made from 10tsp. Hansa yellow light mixed with a scant ⅛tsp. Payne's gray, 10tsp. acrylic glazing liquid, and water in the correct ratio. The flat color consists of 13½oz. (400ml.) black latex flat, 4oz. (120ml.) phthalocyanine blue, and 16tsp. white latex flat. The motif color is made with 1tbsp. white, with ½tsp. Payne's gray and a scant ¼tsp. each cobalt blue and yellow ocher.

❸ FLAME, SLATE, AND ACID YELLOW
The colorwash here is made from 2tbsp. Payne's gray, 1tbsp. white, 3tbsp. acrylic glazing liquid, and water in the correct ratio. The flat paint is a mixture of 17oz. (500ml.) ready-mixed pimento red latex flat and 4tsp. naphthol red. The motif is stamped with 16tsp. Hansa yellow light and ¼tsp. Payne's gray.

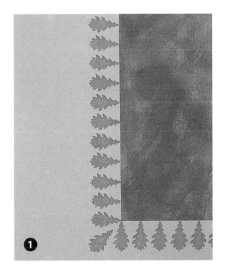

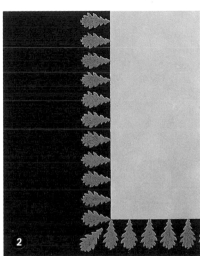

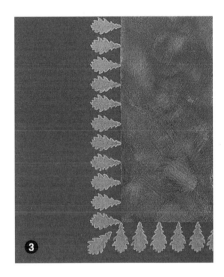

around the area of colorwashing. Mark out the positions of the leaf using the water-soluble marker.

3 Mix the white and Mars red artists' acrylic colors in the screw-top jar to make the leaf color and spoon a little of it onto the ceramic tile. Spread it out with the small roller, then press the stamp into the paint to coat the stamp with an even layer of the color (see page 33).

4 Press the stamp down firmly onto the flat-painted section of wall, making sure that the stamp is at right angles to the line and that the stalk of the leaf is on one of your marks.

5 Continue along the line, recharging the stamp with paint to print each motif.

6 If you are working on a panel design, the corners will appear empty, so you must stamp an extra leaf here. For this extra leaf, position the stamp so that the outer tips of its leaf line up to form a right angle at the corner.

❹ ACID YELLOW, EMERALD, AND TERRA COTTA
Here the colorwash is 5tsp. white with 2½tsp. yellow ocher and 2½tsp. phthalocyanine green, together with 10tsp. acrylic glazing liquid and water in the correct ratio. The flat paint is 17oz. (500ml.) ready-mixed jasmine latex flat, and the motif is 1tbsp. Mars red.

A SIMPLE BORDER

You could paint this border single-handedly, but it would be quicker and more fun to enlist the help of a friend. This will also ensure that, as you proceed along the stripe, you maintain a wet edge while one of you paints and sprays and the other follows up with the sponge to create the texture. If you want to pause, you should do so only at a corner or at a fixture such as a door. If you can foresee that you will have to pause partway along a wall, you should first divide the border into equal lengths using masking tape. You should then complete alternate sections, taking your breaks when a section is painted. When you are ready to start again, mask off the painted sections and fill in the others. The joins between the sections will show, but they will be quite smart and at predetermined intervals.

BASIC RECIPE—BOTTLE GREEN WITH COPPER

PREPARATION

Prepare the surface thoroughly. See pages 26–9.

INGREDIENTS

For a wall 43–54ft.² (4–5m.²) with a border 16ft. x 4in. (5m. x 10cm.)
Background color ▶ 17oz. (500ml.) white latex flat paint / 1 tsp. Payne's gray artists' acrylic color / 1 tsp. raw umber artists' acrylic color / 1 tsp. ultramarine artists' acrylic color
Stripe ▶ 2tsp. phthalocyanine green artists' acrylic color / 2tsp. black artists' acrylic color / 2 tsp. white latex flat paint
Motif ▶ ⅔oz. (20ml.) iridescent copper artists' acrylic color

EQUIPMENT

Container / paint roller plus tray / tape measure / water-soluble marker / string / safe-release masking tape / newspaper / screw-top jar / 1 x 2in. (50mm.) paintbrush / spray bottle / water / 2 cellulose sponges / tracing paper / pencil / flat square eraser / X-Acto knife / ceramic tile / small paint roller

INSTRUCTIONS
Background

Mix the background color in the container. Use the roller to apply 2–3 coats to the wall, allowing 4 hours for each coat to dry, then leave the surface to harden off thoroughly—several days if possible.

L

1 Having decided on the height you would like for the top edge of your border, measure up from the floor, in one corner of the room, or down from the ceiling, to this height (see page 39). Mark lightly on the wall with water-soluble marker. Repeat in the next corner. Stretch a string between these two points, attaching it with masking tape.
2 Stand back and consider this line. Once you are satisfied, stick masking tape both along the string line and 4in.

❶ BOTTLE GREEN WITH COPPER
The basic recipe.

❷ PEWTER WITH FLAX
Here the background color is the same as in the basic recipe, while the stripe is painted with 2oz. (60ml.) iridescent pewter and the motif is stamped with a mixture of 5tsp. white latex flat, 1½tsp. yellow ocher, and ¼tsp. Payne's gray. The iridescent paint used here for the stripe will take longer to dry than the paint used in the basic recipe. You should wait about 5 minutes instead of 2 or 3, before spraying with water.

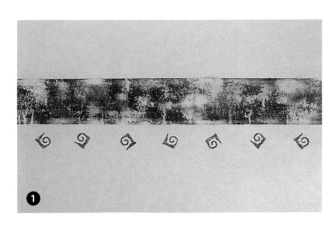

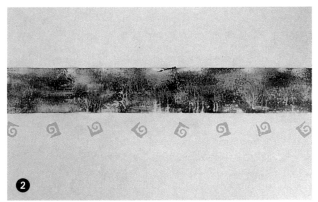

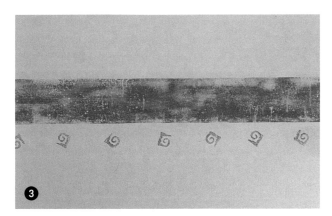

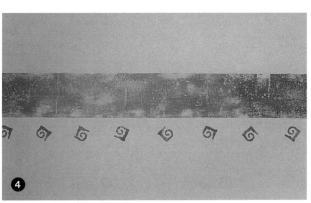

❸ DUSTY MAUVE WITH OLD GOLD
Here the background color is a mixture of 17oz. (500ml.) white latex flat, 5oz. (150ml.) yellow ocher, and 5tsp. Payne's gray. The stripe is painted with 5tsp. white latex flat mixed with ½tsp. dioxazine purple and 2tsp. Payne's gray. The motif is stamped first using ⅔oz. (20ml.) purple, then with ⅔oz. (20ml.) iridescent gold. Leave the iridescent paint to dry before overstamping with the purple.

❹ COPPER WITH DUSTY MAUVE
The background color is the same as in swatch 3, with the stripe painted in 2oz. (60ml.) iridescent copper. The motif uses the purple of the motif of swatch 3. As in swatch 2, the iridescent paint used here for the stripe will take longer to dry than the paint used in the basic recipe.

A SIMPLE BORDER

(10cm.) below it to mark the lower edge of the border. Repeat on each of the walls to be painted. To protect the wall during the next stages, extend the masked-off area with the addition of newspaper above and below the lines of tape.

Stripe

1 Mix the stripe color in the screw-top jar and brush it on to a length of about 1 yard (1 meter) between the lines of tape. Leave to dry for 2–3 minutes.

2 Spray the painted area with water from a plant mister and leave again for 2–3 minutes.

3 Use the sponge to dab the wet surface. Where the water has landed on or run down the surface, the paint will be soft and the sponge will start to lift it off, leaving a textured effect (see pages 51–2).

4 Repeat the spray / wait / dab (and perhaps rub and wipe) procedure until you have achieved the effect you want.

5 Paint the next yard (meter) or so of stripe, joining it gently to the completed section. Repeat the texturing technique with the spray and sponge. This will also allow you to make invisible joins between the sections.

6 As you proceed along the wall, take off the masking tape and remove any color that has seeped behind the tape using a clean, damp sponge. If any of it has dried, wipe off what you can and touch up with the background color.

Motif

1 Trace the design on page 184, enlarge it on a photocopier to the required size, and use it to make the spiral motif rubber stamp (see page 32).

2 Stretch a string, as in Layout, step 1, above, 1in. (2.5cm.) below the stripe.

3 Spoon a little of the motif paint onto a large ceramic tile, roll the paint out using the small roller, and press the stamp into it, just as you would a stamp into an ink pad (see page 33). Stamp the spiral motif along the string line, turning it a little each time as you progress to give the impression that it is spinning along. The spacing between motifs is not critical. You can eyeball it.

STIPPLE & STUCCO

In Part Two, we showed that techniques such as dry brushing and colorwashing, normally used to create an allover texture, can also be applied in blocks or stripes. Stippling can be similarly organized. This not only makes it more manageable to do—especially when you are using water-based paints, which dry quickly—but also visually breaks up the wall with a restrained geometric design.

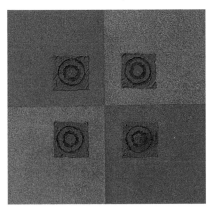

In this instance, we have gone a step further and embossed some of the corners of the blocks with a stenciled modeling-paste motif that is then stamped with powder pigment. The paste has a very light texture, formulated to resemble stucco. It is an excellent complement to the stippling. Some of the colors we have used are quite intense, but overall the design remains simple yet elegant. We would not necessarily decorate every set of corners. In fact, leaving some undecorated would be far more effective. You could, for example, set groups of four embossed corners around a room at random, or you could arrange them at any height along a wall to form a border.

BASIC RECIPE—COBALT BLUE ON MARS RED

PREPARATION

Prepare the surface thoroughly. See pages 26–9.

INGREDIENTS

To cover approximately 43ft.² (4m.²)
Base coat ▶ 10oz. (300ml.) white latex flat paint
Stipple coat ▶ 2tsp. Mars red artists' acrylic color / 2tsp. yellow ocher artists' acrylic color / 6¾oz. (200ml.) acrylic glazing liquid / water in the ratio 1 part color : 10 parts glazing liquid : 3 parts water
Motif ▶ 1tsp. cobalt blue artists' acrylic color / 1tsp. stucco-textured acrylic paste / 1tsp. red iron oxide powder pigment

EQUIPMENT

1 x 8in. (200mm.) medium-textured paint roller plus tray / tape measure / plumb line and/or carpenter's level / water-soluble marker / safe-release masking tape / large container / 1 x 6in. (150mm.) paintbrush / brush for stippling / X-Acto knife / cutting mat / piece of stencil board, 3 x 3in. (8 x 8cm.) / tracing paper / pencil / flat square eraser / palette knife / ceramic tile / repositionable spray adhesive / square of paper

INSTRUCTIONS
Base coats

Use the roller to paint the wall with one or two coats of white latex flat paint. This should leave it opaque white with a slight orange-peel texture. Allow 4 hours to dry between coats, and at least 24 hours before the next stage.

❶ COBALT BLUE ON MARS RED
The basic recipe. The cobalt blue is a fully saturated color, and the addition of the stucco in no way diminishes its intensity. The red iron oxide is equally strong and, being of about the same tone, begins to resonate with the blue. Red iron oxide is also in the stipple color, under the name of Mars red. Such color contrasts can be striking without losing any of their elegance.

❷ MARS RED ON GREEN
In this example, the stucco motif is colored with 1tsp. Mars red and embossed with green metallic powder instead of artists' pigment. The stipple is a cool green made from 2tsp. white, 2tsp. raw umber, and 1tsp. of the powerful phthalocyanine green mixed with 8½oz. (250ml.) glazing liquid and water in the correct ratio.

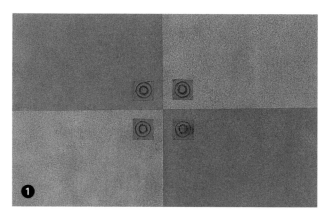

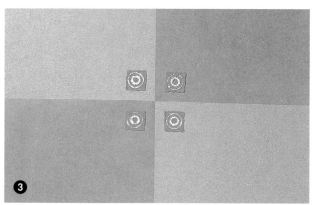

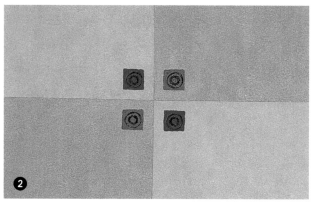

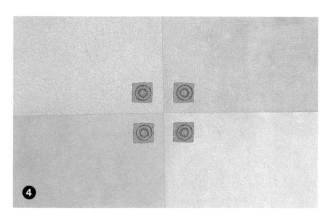

❸ YELLOW OCHER ON PALE BLUE
This background color is even cooler than the green stippled in recipe 2. To make it, dilute 4tsp. white, 1tsp. cobalt blue, and ½tsp. raw umber with glazing liquid and water as before. The stucco-textured modeling paste is colored with 1tsp. yellow ocher and has 1tsp. bright white powder pigment stamped into it.

❹ OCHER ON PARCHMENT
Unlike the other color combinations, this one relies for its effect on tonal and textural contrast, using yellow ochers throughout. The parchment color is made of 4tsp. white, 1tsp. yellow ocher, and a scant ¼tsp. Payne's gray mixed into glazing liquid and water. The stucco-textured modeling paste is colored with 1tsp. yellow ocher and is complemented by the 1tsp. antique gold powder we have stamped into it.

Stipple coat

1 Consider the wall you intend to stipple, and divide it into rectangular or square blocks, marking them out using the tape measure, plumb line and /or level and the water-soluble marker (see page 39). Each block should be no bigger than 16in. (40cm.) along each side. Mask off alternate blocks with masking tape.

2 Mix the stipple coat in the large container. Before applying it to the wall, see pages 58–9. Take note in particular of the short amount of time you will have to work when using water-based paint compared to oil paint. We adopted two strategies to get around this difficulty. The first is to work in small sections, masking out alternate blocks as in Stipple coat, step 1, above. The second is for two people to work in unison. The first worker spreads out the paint with the ordinary paintbrush, while the second follows with the stippling brush. The aim is to maintain a wet edge at all times. Once the paint dries, it will be impossible to stipple it off and create the distinctive soft texture that the technique produces. Two people working together in this way will also substantially shorten the time it takes to cover a wall.

3 Once you have stippled alternate squares, remove the masking tape. Allow to dry (3–4 hours).

4 Mask out the remaining blocks and stipple them in the same way. To achieve the darker tone and create a gentle checkerboard pattern, we stippled the remaining blocks twice, leaving half an hour between coats.

Stucco

1 Use the X-Acto knife to cut a ragged-edged square hole 1½ x 1½in. (4 x 4cm.) in the center of the stencil board, leaving a ¾in. (2cm.) border all around.

2 Trace the motif on page 184, enlarge it on a photocopier, and use it to make a stamp from the eraser (see page 32).

3 Use the palette knife to mix the cobalt blue with the modeling paste on the tile.

4 Spray the back of the stencil lightly with adhesive, and position it with its outer edges aligned with the edges of one of the stippled blocks.

5 Using the palette knife, spread a little of the modeling paste mixture into the stencil. Remove the stencil carefully and repeat in each corner of the stippled block. Let the paste rest for about five minutes while you sprinkle a little of the powder pigment onto a square of paper, then dip the stamp into this powder and press it into the blue, stucco-textured square. The powder prevents the stamp from sticking to the paste, and some remains behind in the indented print.

FLOORS

Painted floors tend to suffer from people's concern that their—or someone else's—handiwork will quickly be damaged, which is fine if you favor the aged look of well-worn medieval church tiles, but not otherwise. To some extent, their fears are well-founded. A painted floor, however well executed and however many layers of varnish you put on top, can never wear as gracefully as natural stone, solid wood, or a tribal rug. But wall-to-wall carpets or sisal do not last forever either—you probably would not want them to—and they can be very expensive to replace.

On the plus side, a painted floor is inexpensive, can be wholly unique, and with today's much improved paints and varnishes is sure to last at least until the urge to redecorate takes hold. In fact, if durability really is a crucial issue, you could choose a paint from one of the types designed specifically for garage or factory floors. They are the toughest floor paints you can buy, intended for use on concrete if necessary, but suitable for other surfaces, too. The color choice is not enormous, but you could mix them or tint them with tinting colors to achieve other hues, or simply work within the existing range, as we did.

Nowadays, most types of floor can be painted. We have painted wooden floorboards, concrete, cork tiles, blockboard, chipboard, and

Above: A warm, ocher-colored country kitchen has a concrete floor whose appearance has been softened by a stenciled petal-in-a-square design.

Left: An Arabic-looking border has been painted around the edge of a wooden floor and is echoed in the paler version that runs along the bottom of the wall. You could do something similar using a mixture of stenciling and freehand painting.

particleboard. Blockboard is perhaps the most neutral of these. We like it because it makes a stable surface for many of our designs. Particleboard is increasingly commonly used for flooring: its main attraction for us is that its slightly textured surface lends itself well to our stone effects. But whatever paint you use, it is often difficult to disguise the true nature of flooring. Floorboards will always be floorboards, no matter what, so, unless you favor the bizarre, don't try to disguise them with false finishes.

Another problem with all these materials is that they will have joints in them which are just not possible to hide. Either ignore them, as we did when we scattered huge stenciled daisies over old floorboards, or try to incorporate the joints into the design—they can conveniently become the joint lines if you are painting a stone-effect floor.

One of the reasons we like painted floors is the scope they offer for bold designs. Whereas we might think twice about covering a wall with checkerboard tiling, we would be more than happy to do the same thing to a floor. So, if a strong graphic look is what you want, you could do worse than apply one to your floor.

If you do decide on a strong design and bold colors, these look best in a sparsely furnished hall or corridor, or up a staircase. Here, the full effect can really be appreciated without any interference from extraneous pieces of furniture. But remember, you do not have to cover a floor completely with a design. There are always odd places where a single motif could be placed. Our *Rose des Vents* could go almost anywhere on a floor so, rather than put it in the center where it may be hidden by a table or a rug, put it where it can be seen.

The following pages include many ideas for painting a floor, but there is one other you could try, especially if your room is a particularly eccentric shape. In this case, it often makes practical and visual sense to confine your painted floor to a ruglike rectangle. And, if you want to add a touch of wit, indulge yourself by painting on some fake tassels or a border to complete the effect.

Below: This room in a New York apartment belongs to an artist who has lovingly decorated it in a style all her own including these unusual geometric painted floorboards with their striking three-dimensional effect.

DAISY-STREWN
FLOORBOARDS

We wanted this floor to look as if it had been strewn with giant flowers. It may look like a difficult project, but there is no need to be discouraged. Thanks to the use of sponging and large, easy-to-use stencils, you could complete it in a day. The arrangement of the flowers is very casual and can be made to fit any shape or size of room. Our flowers are set within a border, which gives the look of a carpet, but one or two small groups of flowers would also be effective. The design is best suited to old floorboards, but it could be used on any floor. A concrete floor, for example, could well benefit from a gentle carpet of flowers, to add a layer of softness to an otherwise austere surface.

BASIC RECIPE—DAISY WHITES ON GREEN

PREPARATION

Prepare the surface thoroughly. See pages 26–9.

INGREDIENTS

For a floor approximately 97ft.² (9m.²)
Basic green ▶ 4oz. (125ml.) white latex flat paint / 1tsp. phthalocyanine green artists' acrylic color / ½tsp. Payne's gray artists' acrylic color / ½tsp. raw umber artists' acrylic color / water in the ratio 2 parts water : 1 part color
Basic gray ▶ 8½oz. (250ml.) white latex flat paint / ¼tsp. Payne's gray artists' acrylic color
Petals ▶ 8tbsp. white artists' acrylic color
Yellow tinge ▶ 4tbsp. basic gray / ½tsp. cadmium yellow medium artists' acrylic color / ½tsp. yellow ocher artists' acrylic color
Mauve tinge ▶ 4tbsp. basic gray / scant ¼tsp. dioxazine purple artists' acrylic color
Blue tinge ▶ 4tbsp. basic gray / scant ¼tsp. ultramarine artists' acrylic color
Flower centers ▶ 5tbsp. Hansa yellow light artists' acrylic color / ¼tsp. Payne's gray artists' acrylic color
Stalks ▶ 8tsp. basic green / ½tsp. Payne's gray artists' acrylic color / ½tsp. phthalocyanine green artists' acrylic color
Border ▶ 8tsp. basic green
Protective coat ▶ 2 liters acrylic or polyurethane floor varnish

EQUIPMENT

Tape measure / straightedge / right-angled triangle / masking tape / newspaper / container / 7 screw-top jars / 1 x 6in. (150mm.) paintbrush / tracing paper / pencil / paper / water-soluble marker / repositionable spray adhesive / stencil board / X-Acto knife / cutting mat / 7 saucers / 4 cellulose sponges and 3 smaller pieces / artists' hog-hair fitch / 1 x 6in. (150mm.) varnish brush

DAISY-STREWN FLOORBOARDS

1 Mark out the perimeter of your design with masking tape. Protect any areas that are not to be painted with newspaper, also taped down.

2 Mix the basic green color in the large container and set aside 16tsp. of it in one of the screw-top jars. Make a colorwash with the remainder in the ratio 1 part water : 2 parts color. Use the ordinary paintbrush to lightly wash color onto the unmasked area. Do not attempt to cover all the wood in one coat—keep it loose and leave some gaps. A second coat will cover any bare wood, but for the best effect, you should deliberately aim for an uneven finish. Allow to dry (2–4 hours).

Layout

1 Trace the designs for the flowers on page 184 and enlarge them as necessary on a photocopier to suit the dimensions of your own floor.

2 Plan your design by scattering the photocopies across the floor until you have a layout you find pleasing, then mark their positions with the marker.

Flowers

1 Use the photocopies to cut your stencils (see page 30), but do not discard the "positives" as you will need them later to act as masks.

2 Spray the back of each flower stencil lightly with adhesive, then place them in position and mask out the centers with their positives.

3 Spoon some of the petal color into one of the saucers and use it to sponge in the flower stencils. You should aim for a soft, misty effect.

4 Round off the ends of three pieces of sponge, to make dabbers about ¾in. (2cm.) across.

❶ DAISY WHITES ON GREEN
The basic recipe. Here the design has been stenciled in the same colors as on page 116, but onto new floorboards, so the colors do not sink in so readily. It has also been varnished with acrylic varnish, which does not darken the wood as much as polyurethane varnish. It also dries very quickly and, being water-based, is safer and more pleasant to use.

5 Mix the basic gray in another screw-top jar and use it as the base for each of the petal tinges. Mix all the remaining colors and store each in its own jar. When you need to use a color, spoon some into a saucer and dab your sponge in it.

6 With the flower stencils still in place and the centers masked out, use the dabbers to apply patches of tinge color (one color per flower) at the inner ends of the petals. Continue across the floor, varying the colors as you go. They do not have to be exactly the same since these are wildflowers. Leave to dry (30–60 minutes).

7 Now position the stencils for the flower centers, masking off the petals with their positives. Sponge the centers in with their color. Do this quite loosely and coarsely. Leave to dry (30–60 minutes).

8 Position the stalk stencil for each flower, placing it at varying angles to create the scattered-flower look, and sponge in with its color.

9 Use the same color to add random flicks of green around the flower centers, applying them with the artists' fitch.

Border

Finally, create the border. To do this, add a line of masking tape 1in. (2.5cm.) in from the tape marking the perimeter. Sponge this border in with the remaining basic green.

Protective coat

Remove all masking and leave to dry for two or three days. Using the varnish brush, apply two or three coats of flat acrylic or polyurethane floor varnish according to the manufacturers' instructions. If you opt for a varnish that requires two chemicals to be mixed together, check that it is compatible with water-based paints.

KIMONOS ON A CONCRETE FLOOR

The challenge in this project was to decorate a floor using standard floor paint without its ending up looking like a garage floor. It was also one of the few occasions when we worked with an oil-based paint. Paint for concrete is easy to apply and creates a very hard surface, though it gives off heavy vapors, so always work in a well-ventilated area. Color choice is restricted, but we opted to work within the available color range rather than attempting to color the paint.

One quart of paint can cover up to 110ft.^{2} (10.3m.^{2}) on a smooth, non-absorbent surface, but considerably less on rough or porous surfaces. Our 150ft.^{2} (14m.^{2}) used over 2½ quarts on its first coat. Subsequent coats spread much farther and were easier to apply.

Our design drew its inspiration from the Japanese kimono, which, when spread out, makes the letter T. In Japanese, the word *kimono* means "wearing thing." Now it is a painted thing. Twelve have gone into our design, laid out flat on the floor to make a rug shape, but clearly you can adjust their number and size to fit your own floor.

The design is painted by hand, following a chalk line. We ruled out the use of masking tape, since the concrete surface was too uneven for the tape. Moreover, the character of the design would have been different had we decided to use tape. Ultimately, we preferred the edge that results from hand-painting. It seemed more in keeping with the Japanese roots of the design.

BASIC RECIPE—BLUE ON NIMBUS GRAY

PREPARATION
Prepare the surface thoroughly. See pages 26–9.

INGREDIENTS
For a floor 150ft.^{2} (14m.^{2}), with a design 9 x 8ft. (2.65 x 2.35m.)
Base coat ► ½–1gal. (2–4 liters) pale gray floor paint
T-shapes ► 17oz. (500ml.) blue floor paint
Bands ► 2tbsp. blue floor paint / 3½oz. (100ml.) brick red floor paint
Motifs ► 2tbsp. slate gray floor paint

EQUIPMENT
1 x 4in. (100mm.) paintbrush / 1 x 3in. (75mm.) paintbrush / tape measure / large right-angled triangle / chalk line / chalk / straight-edge / container / 1 x ¼in. (6mm.) flat artists' brush / 1 x ¾in. (20mm.) flat artists' brush / tracing paper / pencil / paper / repositionable spray adhesive / stencil board

INSTRUCTIONS
Base coat
Using the 4in. (100mm.) paintbrush, apply two coats of the base coat to the entire floor, leaving each coat to dry thoroughly overnight.

KIMONOS ON A CONCRETE FLOOR

Design

1 Using the tape measure, triangle, and chalk line, measure and mark out a rectangle that is 9 x 8 ft. (2.65 x 2.35m.).

2 Using the placement plan below as a guide, measure out each of the T-shaped areas, and mark them lightly in chalk with the aid of a straightedge.

3 Use the 3in. (75mm.) brush to paint them in the appropriate color. Allow to dry overnight.

4 Measure and mark out lightly the 4in. (10cm)-wide bands that run through the center of each T-shape.

5 Mix the paint for these bands in the container and apply to the floor using the ¾in. (20mm.) artists' brush. The bands will need to be left overnight to dry, but if you are careful where you step, you can carry on right away.

Motifs

1 Trace the motif on page 185, enlarge it as necessary on a photocopier, and use it to cut a stencil (see page 30). Use the stencil as a template to draw the motifs at the center of each of their designated spaces. Note how the motifs turn through 90° in alternate squares. Note, too, that at the edges of the design, you only need to draw half the motif. Use the ¼in. (6mm.) artists' brush to paint them in.

2 Leave the floor a good 24 hours before use, but note that it will not be fully hardened until the paint has completely cured, and this can take up to a week.

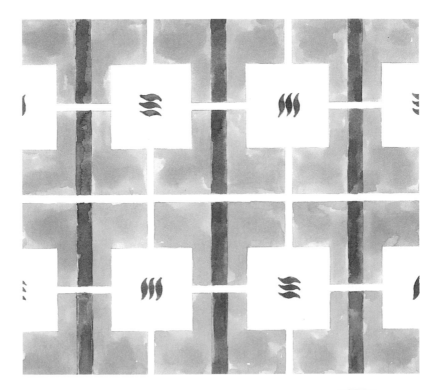

❶ BLUE ON NIMBUS GRAY
The basic recipe. The precision of the layout and the solid color are what the eye is drawn to, while the roughness of the floor acts as a counterpoint.

❷ NIMBUS GRAY ON BLUE
Here the colors have not been changed, just switched around. The kimono shapes and the squiggle motif are in the pale gray painted onto a blue background, while the wide bands are painted in slate gray.

❸ BRICK RED ON SLATE GRAY
In this color combination our kimonos are painted in the brick red floor paint over a slate gray background. The squiggly motifs and the bands are both In the pale gray. Switching colors around in this way can produce quite different results, as a color can become more or less dominant within a design. This is something you could try yourself.

MACKINTOSH-STYLE
STAIRCASE

For this project, we took the set of nine squares that are so much a feature of the work of the early twentieth-century Scottish architect and designer Charles Rennie Mackintosh, and painted them up a flight of stairs and around a landing. The strong rectilinear structure of the design makes for an effect that is crisp and contemporary. We also wish to acknowledge our indebtedness to the inventor of masking tape, since this project, along with many others we have carried out for this book, would have taken a whole lot longer to accomplish if masking tape had not been available.

BASIC RECIPE—DARK GRAY AND STONE

PREPARATION

Prepare the surface thoroughly. Since the risers on a staircase often get kicked, they will benefit from a coat of primer. See pages 26–9.

INGREDIENTS

For a 10-step staircase plus a half-landing
Risers ▶ 10oz. (300ml.) ready-mixed off-white latex flat paint
Border ▶ 6oz. (180ml.) white artists' acrylic color / 3tbsp. raw umber artists' acrylic color / 1tbsp. yellow ocher artists' acrylic color
First square color ▶ 4tbsp. black artists' acrylic color / 2tbsp. white artists' acrylic color / 4tsp. burnt umber artists' acrylic color
Second square color ▶ 2tbsp. white artists' acrylic color / scant ¼tsp. raw umber artists' acrylic color
Protective coat ▶ 1qt. (1 liter) acrylic varnish

EQUIPMENT

1in. (25mm.) safe-release masking tape / paper / X-Acto knife or scissors / 2 x 2in. (50mm.) paintbrushes / 3 screw-top jars / fine-grit sandpaper / tape measure / thin cardboard / pencil / 2 saucers / 2 pieces cellulose sponge / 1 x ¼in. (5mm.) paintbrush / 1 x 3in. (75mm.) varnish brush

INSTRUCTIONS
Risers

Protect the treads with masking tape and paper, then apply two coats of color to the risers using a paintbrush. Allow 4 hours for the first coat to dry, then leave the second coat to dry overnight. Remove the tape and paper.

Border

Using more masking tape, mask off a border, 4½in. (11cm.) wide, down each side of the stairway and around the edge of the half-landing. Mix the border color in a screw-top jar and, again using a paintbrush, apply two coats of paint to the border, allowing 4 hours between coats. Sand down each coat after it has dried, but extend the drying time of the final coat as long as possible. The next stage requires you to use a substantial amount of masking tape, and the harder the paint, the less chance there is of its being lifted off when you remove the tape. We were quite firm with our final sanding, as we wished to create a flat and slightly worn look to this paint layer in order for it to blend in well with the wood of the stairs.

Squares

1 In this design, each riser is decorated with six squares and each tread with nine, all in rows of three. The pattern continues around the landing. Each of the squares is 1¾ x 1¾in. (4.5 x 4.5cm.) and is separated by the width of the masking tape. You may need to adjust the size of your squares to fit the dimensions of the stairway you are working on. Mark out the design using masking tape to create the squares (see page 35). You will need plenty of tape and a lot of time for the masking, but it will be worth the investment of both. You can speed things up by making a "ruler" or template from a strip of thin cardboard, the width of a square. Mark the "ruler" with a row of three squares, spaced and positioned as they will be on the stairs. Use this to mark out the treads and risers for the masking tape. You can make a longer "ruler" to suit the dimensions of your landing.

2 Mix the two colors for all the squares in the remaining screw-top jars. To use each color, place a little of it on a saucer and dab the sponge into it (see page 50). Begin by sponging the first square color on each tread and riser, but leave one square unpainted on each. You should vary the position of these unpainted squares from riser to riser, and from tread to tread. Similarly, as you sponge in the squares around the landing, leave one square unpainted in every block of nine.

3 Once you have finished sponging on the first color, sponge in the unpainted squares using the second square color. This creates a little non-conformity in the otherwise symmetrical design.

4 Remove all the masking tape with care. If any paint has bled beneath the tape, scratch it off with an X-Acto knife and touch it up with a small paintbrush.

5 Allow to dry for two days, protecting the stairway with clean paper if it is in use.

Protective coat

Apply a minimum of three coats of varnish according to the manufacturers' instructions.

❶ DARK GRAY AND STONE
The basic recipe.

❷ STONE AND POWDER BLUE
The risers are as in the basic recipe. The border is 7½oz. (225ml.) white latex flat, 1tbsp. cobalt blue, and 1½tsp. yellow ocher. The first square color is half the border color from the basic recipe, and the second square color is 2tbsp. white, ¼tsp. cobalt blue, ¼tsp. yellow ocher, and ¼tsp. Payne's gray.

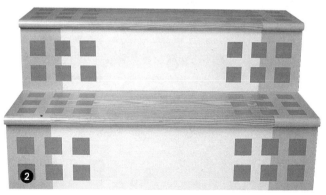

❸ DEEP RED AND DARK SLATE
The risers are as in the basic recipe. The border is 4½oz. (135ml.) black, 4tbsp. white, and 3tbsp. burnt umber. The first square color is 3½oz. (100ml.) naphthol red and 1tsp. Payne's gray. The second square color is 2tbsp. of the border color from the basic recipe.

ROSE DES VENTS

This design, with its stone-finish background, is particularly suited to particleboard. Sometimes laid in panels as a base for other flooring, particleboard is functional but not attractive. You could resist the urge to cover it up, and instead apply our *Rose des Vents*—the poetic French expression for a compass rose. The rough, granular texture of the board lends itself to the stone effect, while the board's panels each become a "slab" of stone. Alternatively, if you do not have a particleboard floor, you could apply the design to a wooden floor, or even to a wall or table top if you wish.

BASIC RECIPE—VENETIAN RED, BLUE, AND GREEN ON SANDSTONE

PREPARATION	**Prepare the surface thoroughly. See pages 26–9.**
INGREDIENTS	*To cover approximately 43–54ft.^{2} (4–5m.^{2})* **Base color ▶ 17oz. (500ml.) white latex flat paint / 5tsp. raw sienna artists' acrylic color** **First glaze coat ▶ 6¾oz. (200ml.) white latex flat paint / 4tsp. raw sienna artists' acrylic color / denatured alcohol** **Second glaze coat ▶ 6¾oz. (200ml.) white latex flat paint / 4tsp. raw sienna artists' acrylic color / 10tsp. raw umber artists' acrylic color / denatured alcohol** **Dabs ▶ 1tsp. raw umber artists' acrylic color / 1tsp. raw sienna artists' acrylic color / 1tsp. Mars red artists' acrylic color** **Medium star ▶ 2tbsp. phthalocyanine green artists' acrylic color / 1tbsp. black artists' acrylic color / 2tsp. yellow ocher artists' acrylic color / 2tsp. white artists' acrylic color** **Circle and small star ▶ 1tbsp. magenta artists' acrylic color / 1tbsp. Mars red artists' acrylic color / 2tsp. white artists' acrylic color** **Large star ▶ 1tbsp. white artists' acrylic color / 1tbsp. cobalt blue artists' acrylic color / ¼tsp. dioxazine purple artists' acrylic color** **Protective coat ▶ 1qt. (1 liter) acrylic floor varnish**
EQUIPMENT	**3 containers / coarse-textured paint roller plus tray / 2 cellulose sponges plus 6 pieces / bowl of water / spray bottle / plate / tracing paper / paper / chalk / hard pencil / 3 screw-top jars / 3 medium flat artists' brushes / 3 small round artists' brushes / fine-grit waterproof sand paper / 1 x 100mm. (4in) varnish brush**
INSTRUCTIONS **Base coats**	Mix the base color in a container and use the roller to apply two coats, allowing 4 hours for each coat to dry.
Stone finish **glazes**	**1** Mix the first glaze coat in another container. Following the instructions for stone finishes on pages 64–5, apply it to the floor using a sponge, adding water, spraying on denatured alcohol, and dabbing on the raw umber, raw sienna, and

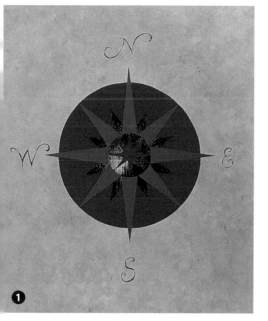

Mars red from the plate. We have sponged the texture in quite evenly, but if you prefer a rugged look to your stone, be a bit freer with the sponge and water.

2 Mix the second glaze coat in the third container and apply it in the same way, again adding in the sponged dabs. Take care not be too heavy-handed. You should aim for a subtle effect. Allow to dry (4 hours).

Motifs

1 Trace the compass design (see page 185), and enlarge it as required on a photocopier. Trace the compass-point initials you require from a book of lettering. The outer circle in our example measures 12¾in. (32cm.) in diameter. Transfer the design to the floor using tracing paper, chalk, and a hard pencil (see page 39), making sure that it is correctly oriented.

2 Mix the stars and circle colors in the screw-top jars. Use the artists' brushes to paint in the center and points of the medium star, then allow to dry (1 hour).

3 Using the sand paper, rub the paint back lightly to reveal parts of the base color as highlights.

4 Now you may well have lost some of your tracing. Retrace as necessary, then paint in the other parts of the design using the appropriate colors and brushes.

5 Finally, use a small round artists' brush to paint the initials of the compass points in the same color as the circle.

Protective coat

Use the varnish brush and follow the manufacturers' instructions to apply a minimum of three coats of varnish.

❶ VENETIAN RED, BLUE, AND GREEN ON SANDSTONE The basic recipe. Here, the small touch of aging on the green star helps push the color back, leaving the red and blue stars looking as if they are floating above it. The colors are in keeping with the period look of the design and lettering.

❷ BLACK AND WHITE ON GRANITE For a granite effect, follow the recipe on page 64. The coloring of the motif is simple: all you will need is 2tbsp. black to paint the large star, and 4tbsp. white for the circle and small star.

CORK-TILE GAMES FLOOR

This design exploits the grid of a cork-tiled floor although it could, of course, be carried out on any suitable surface. We chose eight motifs for stenciling, picked from some well-known board games. Some require two stencils, but none of the designs is complicated. To make the stencils, see page 30. You need not necessarily use all these designs on one floor. For example, repeating the same motif could be very effective. Or, if you favor one game in particular, say Scrabble, it would not be difficult to make your own stencils for a Scrabble floor. Nor do you need to stencil a motif on every square, or even on every other square. The motifs could be centered, dotted around, or marshaled into a border.

We have used mainly latex flat paint. A quart, which would normally cover up to 150ft.^{2} (14m.^{2}) on a smooth wall, may not go so far on cork. It all depends on its texture and absorbency. If you can, test out the paint on a similar surface and estimate from that how much you will need. In principle, though, a 150ft.^{2} (14m.^{2}) floor that is to be painted in a checkerboard pattern will need about a pint of each main color. You will of course require less for the motifs, depending on how many you choose to include.

BASIC RECIPE—CLUB AND LOTTO MARKER

PREPARATION

Prepare the surface thoroughly. See pages 26–9.

INGREDIENTS

For the checkers on a floor approximately 150ft.^{2} (14m.^{2}), choose two of the following:
Cream ► 17oz. (500ml.) white latex flat paint / 4tsp. yellow oxide artists' acrylic color
Maroon ► 15oz. (450ml.) ready-mixed maroon latex flat paint
Black ► 17oz. (500ml.) ready-mixed black latex flat paint
Blue ► 17oz. (500ml.) ready-mixed dark blue latex flat paint

To stencil about 10 motifs, you will need approximately 4tbsp. of one of the above colors. Three are ready-mixed latex paints: the cream is quite simple to mix in small quantities—4tbsp. white latex flat paint with ½tsp. yellow oxide artists' acrylic color.

Protective coat ► ½ gallon (2 liters) acrylic varnish

EQUIPMENT

For the basic recipe
Masking tape / 2 x 3in. (75mm.) paintbrushes / 5 cellulose sponges / 5 saucers / tracing paper / pencil / paper / 3 pieces stencil board, 14½ x 14½in. (38 x 38cm.) / X-Acto knife / cutting mat / repositionable spray adhesive / ruler / 1 x 4in. (100mm.) varnish brush

❶ CLUB AND LOTTO MARKER
The basic recipe uses traditional colors of board games.

❷ SCRABBLE TILE AND CHESS PIECE
This sample uses the same colors as the first, but this time we stenciled onto the maroon-colored squares. The chess piece is a single stencil, while the Scrabble tile is made up of two—a cream square followed by the black-stenciled letter with its tiny numeral.

❸ DOMINO AND CHECKER
Here, the two-part stencils have been stenciled on the cream squares. The first stencil of the domino gives its outline, while the second adds its dots and dividing line. To maintain a neat edge on the tile, mask around it with masking tape before positioning the first stencil and sponging in black. Finish with the second stencil and cream paint. For the checker, center the first stencil—the circle—and sponge in black, then center the second stencil on top and sponge in cream to add the contoured effect.

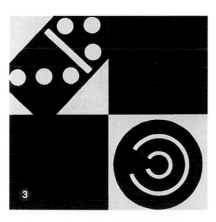

❹ DIE AND BACKGAMMON
Both the die and the backgammon motif are made from single stencils on cream squares. For neat edges for both, mask around their squares with masking tape before you position the stencils. The die is the one stencil that can be placed at any angle, and you could vary this in each square as you work across your floor to give an appearance of movement within the design. The die is both mask and stencil. Stencil around its edge in black, then complete by adding dots in blue. For the backgammon, sponge the outer sections in black and the central section in blue.

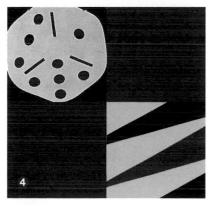

CORK-TILE GAMES FLOOR

INSTRUCTIONS
Checkerboard

1 Mask off around the edges of alternate tiles to guarantee sharp edges, then paint in cream. Apply the paint with one of the paintbrushes, and follow up with a sponge to create an even texture. Remove the masking tape, allow to dry (2 hours), and repeat.

2 Mask around the edges of the cream tiles, and paint the remainder in maroon, using the same technique.

Stencils

1 Trace the club and lotto motifs from the photographs and scale them up on a photocopier so they fit your tiles. The lotto motif is made up of two stencils. The first gives the circle, and the second the number.

Most cork tiles are 12in. (30cm.) square. To help position the stencils in the exact center of each tile when stenciling, cut the three pieces of stencil board 1¼in. (3cm.) larger all around than a tile. Pencil in the diagonals on each stencil and at their corners, mark out and remove a 1¼in. (3cm.) square. When you come to position the stencils, these notches will enable you easily to align their corners with those of the tiles. Attach the scaled-up motifs to the center of each piece of stencil board, using the diagonals as a guide. Cut with an X-Acto knife to make the three stencils (see page 30).

2 To stencil the club motif, spray the back of the stencil with adhesive and position it on a cream square. Sponge in black, applying the color quite densely but leaving the edges slightly uneven (see page 31). The texture left by the sponge will complement the natural texture of the cork. Remove the stencil and allow to dry (30–60 minutes).

3 To stencil the lotto marker, first spray the back of the circle stencil with adhesive, position it on a cream square, and sponge in black, as in step 2 above. Remove the stencil, allow to dry (30–60 minutes), then position the number stencil and sponge in cream.

Protective coat

Use the varnish brush to apply a minimum of three coats of varnish according to the manufacturers' instructions.

MOSAIC BORDER

Painting a mosaic might seem a time-consuming business at first glance, but using a set of foam-rubber stamps can speed things up considerably. We have confined this design to a border on a floor, but if you are more ambitious, you could cover the whole floor in a similar way. With careful planning you can make your border go around corners and into alcoves, or you could set it as a rectangle or square, regardless of the shape of your room. You could also of course, easily run this border along a wall.

If you apply the border to a floor, the smoother and flatter the floor, the easier it will be to print. We have used ¾in. (2cm.)-thick plywood as our base. This takes a water-based wood stain very well, and the stain can subsequently be painted over without any problem using acrylic paints. If you like the idea of the mosaic but have a different floor surface, then alter the background accordingly. Particleboard, for example, could be given a stone finish (as for the *Rose des Vents* on pages 128–9). Floorboards might seem an unlikely site for a mosaic, but if you have new, featureless boards, a mosaic might prove to be the quirky idea that will bring them to life.

BASIC RECIPE—BLACK AND WHITE ON UMBER

PREPARATION

Prepare the surface thoroughly. See pages 26–9.

INGREDIENTS

For a border approximately 33ft. (10m.) long
**Background ▶ Umber water-based floor stain. See manufacturers' instructions for quantity required for your floor.
Base coat ▶ 10oz. (300ml.) white latex flat paint / 2tbsp. raw umber artists' acrylic color
First mosaic color ▶ 5oz. (150ml.) white artists' acrylic color
Second mosaic color ▶ 3tbsp. black artists' acrylic color / 1tbsp. phthalocyanine blue artists' acrylic color / 2tsp. white artists' acrylic color
Protective coat ▶ acrylic floor varnish. See manufacturers' instructions for quantity required for your floor.**

EQUIPMENT

1 x 4in. (100mm.) paintbrush / medium-grit sandpaper /tape measure / ruler / graph paper / pencil / chalk line or string / masking tape / cash register tape / container / 3 small paint rollers / 1 paint tray / 3 ceramic tiles / 4 foamcore backing boards: 2 of 7 x 7in. (18 x 18cm.); 1 of 2½ x 2½in. (6 x 6cm.); 1 triangular piece 2½ x 1½ x 1½in. (6 x 4 x 4cm.) / 1 piece foam-rubber mat 5½ x 8in. (14 x 20cm.) / X-Acto knife / cutting mat / tube paper cement / 2 screw-top jars / newspaper / 1 x 4in. (100mm.) varnish brush

MOSAIC BORDER

INSTRUCTIONS
Background

Using the paintbrush and following the manufacturers' instructions, give the floor one or two coats of stain as required. Sand lightly after each coat with the sandpaper.

Border

The 7in. (18cm.)-wide border consists of two alternating 7in. (18cm.)-square motifs. Plan the position of your border on the floor. In a perfect world, each length of border would divide exactly into an odd number of squares, but the chances of this are slim. With the aid of graph paper and a little forethought, though, you can plan for the best possible layout. If you are unable to fit in all the squares exactly, it will not be too serious a problem. When printing, you will be starting from a corner and working along a side to its mid-point, which is where the problem will be resolved (see Printing, step 2 below).

Set out the border on the floor with a chalk line or string, and mask off the surrounding area with tape and cash register tape.

Base coat

Mix the base coat color in the large container, and apply the paint to the border using a small roller. Some of this base coat will show through between the mosaics as grout, so ensure a good coverage. Give it two coats if necessary.

Stamps

1 Make up the four individual stamps used in the design (see page 32). The two main stamps—the crosses—are 7in. (18cm.) square. For these, draw a grid of ¾in. (2cm) squares on the first 7 x 7in. (18 x 18cm.) backing board. Draw a similar grid, but this time set out on the diagonal, on the other 7 x 7in. (18 x 18cm.) board. (Note that if you work in inches, you will need to make the squares ever so slightly larger than ¾in. to fill the space.) Cut the foam mat up into ⅝in. (1.7cm.) squares, and glue these with clear paper cement to the backing boards to form the two crosses. You will also need a few small triangular pieces of foam to complete the diagonally placed cross.

2 Using the small square backing board and the triangular piece, make the other two stamps in the same way.

Printing

1 Mix the first and second mosaic colors in the jars. To print the border, begin with the two crosses. Place a spoonful or two of the first color on a tile, then transfer some to the stamp with a roller. Test the stamp out before you start. This will let you see if the design is printing well, and will allow you to gauge how much paint to roller on, and how much

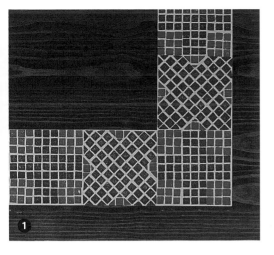

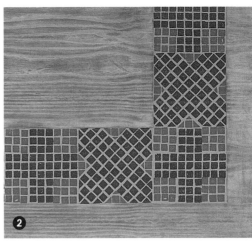

❶ GREEN AND TERRA COTTA ON MAHOGANY
Here we used a more traditional wood coloring—in this case a mahogany stain—for the background. The red mosaic is mixed from 3tbsp. magenta, 3tbsp. Mars red, and 2tbsp. white, while the green mosaic is made using 4tsp. white, 4tsp. phthalocyanine green, and 1tsp. Payne's gray.

pressure to apply. Press the stamp down firmly, but not so hard that paint squeezes out sideways.

Once you are confident that you have the knack, begin at a corner, printing alternate crosses as you go. As you approach the center of the side, switch to the opposite corner and work along from there, starting with the same cross as before.

2 If you are unable to finish the side with a complete cross, then make sure that the last prints on each side of the center line are of the same pattern.

You now have to fill the remaining space with a motif that may be larger or smaller than a complete print. To do this, place a sheet of newspaper beyond the center, along a line that gives half the width of a "grout" line. The newspaper will act as a mask and will not allow you to print beyond this center line. Print the next cross butted up to the last, but overlapping the newspaper. Remove the newspaper and allow this print to dry for 5–10 minutes.

3 Place a fresh sheet of paper over this last print and again along a line half a grout width beyond the center line. Print the motif in the remaining space. Remove the paper to reveal a symmetrical center motif.

Alternatively, you could design a completely new stamp for this space—for example, a series of vertical stripes or a stamp with your initials.

4 Complete the design in the same way with the second mosaic color and the two remaining stamps.

❷ BLUE AND OCHER ON PALE BLUE
The ready-mixed floor stain is in one of the brighter colors that are now available and has been used as a background for a border with a Mediterranean coloring. For the blue, we mixed 4tbsp. cobalt blue with 4tbsp. white and 1tsp. Payne's gray. The contrasting mosaics are in 3–4tbsp. yellow ocher.

Protective coat Leave to dry for at least 24 hours. Then, using the varnish brush, apply a minimum of three coats of varnish according to the manufacturers' instructions.

GRAINED FLOOR

This is a development of the graining design illustrated on page 53, but in it we make use of more subdued color schemes. You will need to start with a smooth floor—one made of thick plywood, for example. We envisioned using the design to cover a floor from wall to wall, although you could easily adapt it to make a border for a floor or even an allover design for a table top.

BASIC RECIPE—TURQUOISE AND EGGPLANT

PREPARATION

Prepare the surface thoroughly. See pages 26–9.

INGREDIENTS

For a floor approximately 54ft.² (5m.²)
First color ▶ 1¼qt. (1.2 liters) white latex flat paint / 10oz. (300ml.) neutral gray artists' acrylic color / 1tbsp. phthalocyanine green artists' acrylic color
Second color ▶ 20oz. (600ml.) raw umber artists' acrylic color / 7½oz. (225ml.) neutral gray artists' acrylic color / 7½oz. (225ml.) dioxazine purple artists' acrylic color
Protective coat ▶ 1½qt. (1.5 liters) flat acrylic floor varnish

EQUIPMENT

2 containers / 2 paint rollers plus trays / cardboard / metal ruler / pencil / X-Acto knife / cutting mat / chalk line / water-soluble marker / 2in. (50mm.) masking tape / 2½in. (60mm.) cash register tape / scissors / repositionable spray adhesive / paper / safe-release masking tape / 1 x 2in. (50mm.) paintbrush / graining rocker / 1 x 4in. (100mm.) varnish brush or roller

INSTRUCTIONS
Background

Mix the first color in a container, and paint the floor with two coats, using the roller. Allow 2–4 hours between coats, and leave overnight after the second coat.

Squares

1 Cut a 2½in. (6cm.) square hole at the center of a 12in. (30cm.) square piece of cardboard. Cut another piece of cardboard 3½ x 12in. (90 x 30cm.). With the aid of these templates, the marker, and a chalk line, mark out a grid of 12in. (30cm.) squares separated by 3½in. (9cm.) spaces across the whole floor. Use the 2in. (5cm.) masking tape to mask out the spaces.
2 Mix the second color in another container, and use a roller to paint the squares with two coats of this color, allowing 4 hours for each coat to dry.
3 Cut the cash register tape into as many squares as you have painted. Spray one side of each of these with adhesive, and set them at the center of each painted square, using the square cardboard template as a guide.

❶ TURQUOISE AND EGGPLANT
The basic recipe.

❷ CREAM AND SLATE BLUE
The first color is 1¼qt. (1.2 liters) white, 2¾oz. (80ml.) Hansa yellow light, and 2¾oz. (80ml.) raw umber. The second color is 20oz. (600ml.) cobalt blue, 6¾oz. (200ml.) Mars black, and 6¾oz. (200ml.) white.

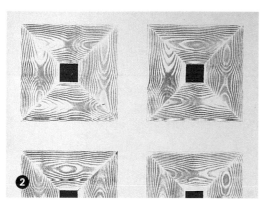

4 Cut plenty of 12in. (30cm.) squares of paper each into four triangles.

5 Using the safe-release masking tape, in conjunction with the triangles cut from the paper, mask off opposite sections of each of your squares completely along the diagonals, leaving the two other sections exposed. Hold down the bottom edge of the paper triangles with another piece of masking tape.

❸ BRONZE AND SLATE BLUE
The first color is a ready-mixed light bronze latex flat paint. The square is painted in a mixture of 30oz. (900ml.) white and 5oz. (150ml.) neutral gray, while the graining color is 1qt. (1 liter) of the second color from swatch 2.

Graining

1 Using the paintbrush and the first color, paint in the two exposed sections fairly thickly. Immediately drag the rocker across the wet paint to create the graining pattern (see page 53). Remove the paper triangles and the masking tape, and allow to dry (at least 4 hours).

2 Mask out for the remaining two sections of each square and repeat step 1 above, then very carefully remove all the masking. Leave to harden (1–2 days).

Protective coat

Using the varnish brush and following the manufacturers' instructions, apply at least three coats of varnish.

DOORS & WINDOWS

One of the biggest attractions for us of decorating a door or window is that it provides a frame to work within or around. This immediately gives us somewhere to anchor our design and give it a shape—a reassuring thought even for a professional—but without its being restricting. In fact, confining a design to a door panel or to the area around a window is liberating: you can be adventurous with shape and color in a way that would be overpowering and inappropriate for a whole wall.

This is nothing new. Architects have long focused attention on doors—especially on front doors—and on windows. The front porches of Gothic cathedrals provide an exuberant display of stonework, a visual *aide-mémoire* of the building's purpose, while

magnificent stained-glass windows add their ethereal message to the story. In the same way, the entrances to palaces, stately homes, theaters, and opera houses also make the statement that, by passing through them we are about to leave the ordinary world and enter a place of mystery, power, or make-believe.

You, too, can decorate your doors and windows with a promise of things to come. The heavy symbolism of a cathedral would not necessarily be appropriate for your living room, but you can borrow from these ideas, painting a kitchen cabinet door, as we did, with a fruit or vegetable motif to reflect the domestic activity that goes on in that part of your home. Or, moving into the realm of wishful thinking, you could paint a window so the light filtering through has the glow of permanent sunshine, or a door so it reminds you of a weatherbeaten

Above: Concentrating a design on a window frame allows you to indulge in strong imagery while leaving the walls free for pictures. Here, at Charleston in Sussex, England, the shape of the window recess makes an ideal place for some painted decoration.

Left: This doorway has been given a very individualistic look, with motifs from the Orient beckoning us to enter the room.

beach hut and happy summer days spent relaxing by the sea.

Another attraction of painting doors and windows—including the window opening and sometimes some of the surrounding wall as well—is that they are ideal starting points to try out decorative paintwork without committing yourself to the makeover of a whole room.

But if you are decorating a whole room, many ideas in this book would make excellent foils for your doors and windows. For instance, the Seaweed and Shell Closet is complemented by aging on the surrounding paneling. Colorwashed walls would work well with our Whimsical Window Frame, while the Late-Summer Seedhead Frieze would look perfect with windows painted in complementary colors. And, although our designs were intended for doors and windows, you could adapt them for use elsewhere—on archways or fireplaces, for example. As before, we provide you with the tools. You must have the courage to let your imagination run free.

Left: Door panels and architraves can provide an anchor for a design. The decoration on these old, richly colored doors looks complex, but conslsts of nothing more than simple flower designs linked together to make borders.

SEAWEED AND
SHELL CLOSET

Milk paints would be attractive for these closet doors, and if you have an old house and wish to use traditional paints, they would be the ideal choice. Also called casein paints, they are not widely available, but many manufacturers make an acrylic-based, matte-finish paint that could be used in their place. We have chosen ours from a line developed to look like milk paint in finish and color, and we found it a successful alternative. Whether it will be as durable as the real thing remains to be seen.

BASIC RECIPE—ANTIQUE WHITE WITH SAGE

PREPARATION

Prepare the surface thoroughly. See pages 26–9.

INGREDIENTS

For 3 large closet doors
**First color ▶ 10oz. (300ml.) sage "milk" paint
Second color ▶ 10oz. (300ml.) antique white "milk" paint
Third color ▶ 1tsp. dioxazine purple artists' acrylic color / 1tsp neutral gray artists' acrylic color
Border squares ▶ ¾tsp. phthalocyanine green artists' acrylic color / 1½tsp. neutral gray artists' acrylic color / 1tsp. white artists' acrylic color**

EQUIPMENT

2 x 2in. (50mm.) decorators' brushes / 2 x 4in. (100mm.) paintbrushes / tracing paper / pencil / paper / 3 pieces stencil board / repositionable spray adhesive / X-Acto knife / cutting mat / tape measure / water-soluble marker / 3 saucers / 2 cellulose sponges plus 2 rounded-off pieces / fine-grit sand paper / bucket of water / 1 x ¼in. (6mm.) square-ended artists' brush / tiny, fine natural sponge

INSTRUCTIONS
Background

1 Using the decorators' brushes, apply two coats of the first color to the doors. Begin with the panels, then follow up by painting first the cross rails, then the stiles. Finish each section by brushing out the paint in the same direction as the grain. We have also painted the paneling surrounding the doors. Allow 1–2 hours for each coat to dry.
2 Apply two coats of the second color in the same way.

SEAWEED AND SHELL CLOSET

Stencils

1 Trace the designs on page 185, enlarge as necessary, and use to make the first stencil—the wavy rectangles with the seaweed—and the second stencil—the registration marks and the shell motifs (see page 30).

2 Position the first stencil in the center of the door panel, holding it in place with the spray adhesive. Sponge on some of thr first color using a trimmed cellulose sponge (see page 31). Remove the stencil and repeat the process on the other doors. Leave the paint to dry overnight.

3 Using very fine sand paper with water, lightly sand the doors, including the stenciled areas and the moldings. Avoid removing too much paint from the stenciled areas, and do not sand the paint back beyond the first color (see pages 54–5). Rinse the sand paper frequently in a bucket of water, and use a sponge to mop up the slurry of paint. Clean up well with a fresh sponge and plenty of clean water.

4 Position the second stencil on one of the doors, using the registration marks to line it up with the first stenciled motifs. Sponge on the second color, again using a trimmed cellulose sponge, and applying the color a little unevenly to create highlights. Remove the stencil and allow to dry (2 hours). Repeat on the other doors.

5 Cut out from the third piece of stencil board the registration marks and the line details of the shells (see page 185). Do not cut the lines for the border for the moment. Position this stencil over the already-stenciled motifs, lining it up with the registration marks on each corner.

6 Mix the third color on a saucer, using an artists' brush to blend the paints together. Using a tiny natural sponge (synthetic ones are too coarse), stencil in the details—not too evenly—with this color. Remove the stencil and allow to dry (30 minutes). Repeat on the other doors.

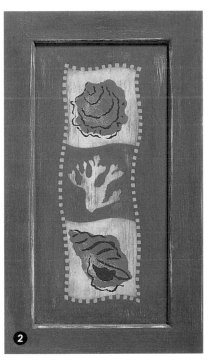

❶ ANTIQUE WHITE WITH SAGE
The basic recipe. The antique white and pale sage green showing through suit this room beautifully, giving it a Scandinavian air.

❷ SKY BLUE WITH ANTIQUE WHITE
Here we have painted two coats of sky blue "milk" paint—a total of 10oz. (300ml.)—over two coats of antique white— also 10oz. (300ml.) The third color, for the stencil details, is a mixture of 1½tsp. white and ¼tsp. each burnt sienna and burnt umber. The border squares are in 4tsp. white plus ¼tsp. phthalocyanine green.

❸ PRIMROSE YELLOW WITH EGGPLANT
We began with 10oz. (300ml.) eggplant "milk" paint, followed by 10oz. (300ml.) primrose yellow. The third color is a mixture of 1½tsp. white and ¼tsp. each phthalocyanine blue and neutral gray. The border squares are a lighter version of these colors, made by doubling the quantity of white.

Border

1 Cut the lines for the border out of the third stencil. Reposition this, and use as a template to draw in the border.

2 Mix the border squares color on a saucer, and use a square-ended artists' brush to paint in the small squares between the marked border lines. Make sure that you end up with a square in each corner.

PAINTED PANES ON
A PART-GLAZED DOOR

If you are looking for an alternative to glass curtains or Venetian blinds, painting a window may be the answer. It can be more than just a device to distract your eye when there is a less-than-pretty view on the other side. Painting a window is also a lovely way to filter the light that passes through it, and on bright sunny days, the colors of the paint will be projected into the room, which can be uplifting, summer or winter. A painted interior glass door will also give a room color that changes as the daylight fades and lamps are turned on.

The windows on these pages were decorated with a paint designed to give the appearance of colored or stained glass. It was bought from an artists' supplier. Once it has hardened, you can clean the glass with a soft cloth, but use only the mildest of detergents.

We wanted to stencil the design and found the best material to make the stencil was self-adhesive plastic film attached to the glass before the motifs were cut out from it. It sticks firmly to the glass, but can be removed easily. We had first tried using acetate and met with some success, but even though the acetate was attached with spray adhesive, the very liquid paint seeped underneath, leaving us with a very messy clean-up operation.

After painting the glass, we chose a harmonizing yellow color to paint the door frame.

BASIC RECIPE—SKY BLUE AND OLIVE

PREPARATION

Prepare the surfaces thoroughly. See pages 26–9.

INGREDIENTS

For an average window
First color ▸ 1¾oz. (50ml.) sky blue glass paint
Second color ▸ 1¾oz. (50ml.) olive green glass paint
Door frame ▸ 5tbsp. white latex flat paint / 2tbsp. yellow ocher artists' acrylic color / 3tbsp. Hansa yellow light artists' acrylic color / 2tsp. raw umber artists' acrylic color

EQUIPMENT

Tracing paper / pencil / paper / clear acetate (optional) / glue stick / repositionable spray adhesive / transparent self-adhesive plastic film / X-Acto knife / masking tape / 2 saucers / 2 small, rounded-off pieces cellulose sponge / container / 1 x 2in. (50mm.) paintbrush / 1 x 1in. (25mm.) paintbrush

INSTRUCTIONS
Layout

1 Trace the spiral and leaf motifs on page 186 and enlarge them on a photocopier, making several copies. Arrange them into a design that will fit your door. On our door, we decorated a top and bottom row of panes. Each pane was

divided into three equal bands, with the motifs in each reversed from pane to pane. To make the reversed motifs, photocopy them onto acetate and turn the copies over. If acetate is not available, tape photocopied motifs back to front on a window, and pencil over the image seen. On our door, the upper panes had leaves in the top two bands and spirals in the lower band. The lower panes had spirals in the top band and leaves in the lower two bands. The instructions that follow are for panes with spirals in the top band.

2 Once you have planned your design, glue the individual motifs in position on a sheet of paper that fits your panes, and attach to the glass with a light spray of adhesive.

Stencil

1 Cut pieces of transparent self-adhesive plastic film to the exact size of your window panes, and attach them to the front of the glass. This plastic film is to become your stencil.

2 Using an X-Acto knife, cut carefully along the lines of the design as seen through the glass. (A word of caution: The point of the knife will leave lines scratched on most types of glass. These will not be visible after the painting, as the edges of the paint will coincide with them, but if you decide subsequently to remove the paint, they will show. To prevent this, you can cut the stencils from the plastic film before you stick it down, but be warned that this is a much more tricky procedure.)

3 Peel away the following sections of the stencils: from the lower band, peel off the background, leaving the leaf shapes in place; from the middle band, peel away the leaves, leaving the background in place; from the top band, peel away the background, leaving the spirals in place. You will now be left with a stencil attached to your glass, which the sign-painter's paint cannot get behind.

4 Protect the door frame around the glass with masking tape, then starting with the middle band, also mask off below the leaf stems to prevent the color from seeping into the lower band.

5 Pour a little of the first color into a saucer. Use a small piece of sponge to apply it to the leaves in the middle band. Sponge the color out, working continuously until you have an even texture (see pages 66–7). Allow to dry (4 hours).

6 Remove the masking from below the stems, and protect the work you have just completed with masking tape laid

❶ SKY BLUE AND OLIVE The basic recipe. This rather Mediterranean color combination would bring a warm glow to any room.

❷ GRAY AND TURQUOISE Here the central leaves have been stenciled in gray sign-painter's paint, and the two outer bands in turquoise. To make the color for the door frame, mix ½tsp. each phthalocyanine green and burnt umber into 6oz. (180ml.) white latex.

delicately across stems and leaf tips, where they touch the top and bottom bands.

7 Pour a little of the second color into a saucer, and with a fresh piece of sponge apply it to the top and bottom bands, sponging out as before. Allow to dry (4 hours).

8 Remove the plastic-film stencils and masking tape from the door frame to reveal your design crisply painted on the glass. At this stage it will still be a little delicate, but it becomes harder after a few days.

Door frame Mix the paint for the door frame in the container and use the paintbrushes to apply two coats, allowing 2–4 hours for each coat of paint to dry.

ARTICHOKE
CABINETS

Being both a flower and a vegetable, the artichoke makes a very apt motif for anyone who wants to give a country feel to his or her kitchen cabinets. It is also, happily, a very suitable shape for decorating a cabinet door. By making the artichoke design into a stencil, you can easily repeat it a number of times on different doors, while the technique of rubbing-off will bring a little individuality to each one. In our choice of design we must acknowledge our debt to the style of Charleston, that gloriously decorated house in Sussex, England, belonging to Vanessa Bell and Duncan Grant. In the first half of the twentieth century, these two artists, painted almost every surface of their home with organic and abstract motifs.

BASIC RECIPE—SAGE ON CARMINE

PREPARATION

Prepare the surface thoroughly. See pages 26–9.

INGREDIENTS

For 4-5 standard cabinet doors
Base color ▶ 10oz. (300ml.) magenta artists' acrylic color / 1tbsp. Mars red artists' acrylic color / 1tbsp. naphthol red artists' acrylic color Second color ▶ 3½oz. (100ml.) white artists' acrylic color / 10tsp. cobalt blue artists' acrylic color / 5tsp. yellow ocher artists' acrylic color

EQUIPMENT

2 containers / smooth paint roller plus tray / tape measure / paper / repositionable spray adhesive / 1 x 3in. (75mm.) paintbrush / cotton cloth / bowl of water / 4 cellulose sponges / tracing paper / pencil / paper / stencil board / X-Acto knife / cutting mat / 2 saucers / water-soluble marker / small artists' brush

INSTRUCTIONS
Base coats

1 Mix the base color in one of the containers, then use the roller to apply two coats, allowing 2 hours between coats and 4 hours after the second coat.

2 Mask off a 2in. (5cm.) border around the edge of each of the doors using torn strips of paper attached with a light spray of adhesive.

3 Mix the second color in the other container, then use the brush to apply a coat of this color, brushing it on in a vertical direction. Leave this to barely dry—10–15 minutes and maybe less on a hot day.

4 Remove the paper mask. You must now work rapidly and

with some vigor, rubbing the painted surface firmly with the cloth dampened in water (see pages 48–9). Work in the same direction as the brush strokes. Wash the cloth out frequently, and rub until you have achieved an effect similar to that in the photographs. Clean up the border with a damp sponge.

Stencils

1 Trace the motifs on page 186, enlarge them on a photocopier, and use them to make the two stencils for the artichoke (see page 30).

2 Center the silhouette stencil on the door. If your door is very tall, leave a slightly deeper space at the bottom of the stencil than at the top, or the artichoke will look as though it is slipping downward. Hold it in position with a spray of adhesive. Spoon some base color into a saucer, then sponge it on. Remove the stencil and allow to dry (30 minutes).

3 Position the second stencil over the silhouette, fix it with adhesive in the same way, and sponge on the second color. Do not attempt to get the paint surface too flat or you will lose some of the character of the piece. Remove the second stencil and allow to dry (30 minutes).

Border

Using the water-soluble marker and the tape measure, measure and mark out the border of diagonal lines spaced at ¾in. (2cm.) intervals. Paint the lines freehand using the artists' brush. Have a bowl of clean water on hand while you are painting, together with a sponge to wipe away any drips or errant lines. As you paint the lines, gently press on them with the sponge to soften them. Do this on three or four lines at a time, as soon as they are painted. If any marker shows once the lines are finished, it can be washed off with the damp sponge after the paint has dried.

❶ **SAGE ON CARMINE**
The basic recipe. Our first color choice contrasts red with green. Such coloring is well suited to pepping up a drab corner but may be too strong for some people's taste.

❷ WEDGWOOD ON INDIAN YELLOW
A second possibility is to start with a yellow base coat made of 10oz. (300ml.) Hansa yellow light, 3½oz. (100ml.) yellow ocher, and a little Payne's gray on the tip of a teaspoon. The rubbed-back color is a pale blue of almost the same tone. This is a mixture of 6¾oz. (200ml.) white with 4tsp. each of cobalt blue and Payne's gray.

❸ WEDGWOOD ON SAGE
Here the pale green from the basic recipe is used as the base color, with the blue of swatch 2 rubbed back on top. The first stencil is sponged in the green, while the second uses a third color—a dark green made of 2tsp. each black, white, and phthalocyanine green. As a further embellishment, we have dabbed in a few touches of the red with which we began our first cabinet.

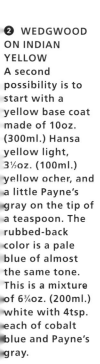

WHIMSICAL WINDOW FRAME

The design for this window frame has four unequal sections, each one wrapped around the corner of the window opening. The overlapping shapes are created by masking with torn paper and masking tape. Where the overlaps occur, a darker area results, which we have stenciled with a diamond motif. The outer edge of the design is masked entirely using torn paper, but where sections overlapped, we masked one of the edges with masking tape to give a straight edge.

You can, of course, adapt a project like this to suit any size or shape of window, and we recommend that if you are decorating more than one window in a room, you should vary the masking from window to window to avoid a regimented appearance.

BASIC RECIPE—RASPBERRY, SALMON, AND PEA GREEN

PREPARATION — Prepare the surface thoroughly. See pages 26–9.

INGREDIENTS — *For an average window and the area surrounding it*
Background ▸ 17oz. (500ml.) ready-mixed pale dusty pink latex flat paint
First color ▸ 6tbsp. white latex flat paint / 2tbsp. cadmium yellow artists' acrylic color / 1½tsp. cobalt blue artists' acrylic color / 1½tsp. raw umber artists' acrylic color / acrylic glazing liquid and water (see instructions)
Second color ▸ 3½oz. (100ml.) white latex flat paint / 2tsp. raw umber artists' acrylic color / 2tsp. Mars red artists' acrylic color / acrylic glazing liquid and water (see instructions)
Third color ▸ 4tbsp. white latex flat paint / 4tbsp. magenta artists' acrylic color / 2tsp. raw umber artists' acrylic color / 2tsp. raw sienna artists' acrylic color / acrylic glazing liquid and water (see instructions)

EQUIPMENT — Masking tape / medium-textured paint roller plus tray / small, fine-textured paint roller plus tray / 6 x 3in. (75mm.) paint-brushes / 1 x 2in. (50mm.) paintbrush / 3 x 1in. (25mm.) paintbrushes / paper / tape measure / repositionable spray adhesive / 3 screw-top jars / 3 large, deep plates

INSTRUCTIONS — 1 Mask off the window frame with masking tape.
Background — 2 Using the medium paint roller and the medium paintbrush for the corners, paint the surrounding wall and the window opening with the background color.

Masking — 1 Begin at the bottom right-hand corner by masking with a

vertical strip of torn paper on the face of the wall, 4–6in. (10–15cm.) away from the window opening (see pages 34–5). Attach with a light spray of adhesive. Run a horizontal line of masking tape across the face of the wall and into the window opening to finish this area of masking with a straight line.

2 Mask beneath the window with a band of torn paper running across the sill and down the face of the wall below the window. Take it down to the baseboard if you wish.

3 Mask off the top left-hand section in a similar manner, again using a torn-paper mask, its lower edge finished with a straight, horizontal line of masking tape.

Painting

1 Mix the first color in a screw-top jar, and use the small roller in conjunction with a 1in. (25mm.) paintbrush to paint the bottom right-hand section. Apply two coats, allowing 2–4 hours for each coat to dry.

2 Dilute 1tbsp. first color with an equal amount of glazing liquid plus 4tbsp. water on a deep plate. Use a 3in. (75mm.) brush to colorwash the masked-off upper left-hand section, and brush off with a clean, soft 3in. (75mm.) brush and a 1in. (25mm.) brush for the corners (see pages 44–5). Apply a second coat of colorwash, allowing 2 hours between coats. Remove all the masking, but leave it in place at the top left-hand corner as more coats of paint are to be applied here.

❶ LILAC, SIENNA, AND CREAM OVER GARNET
Here the background is 17oz. (500ml.) ready-mixed terra cotta red latex flat. The first color is 5tbsp. white latex flat, plus 1¼tsp. raw umber and 2½tsp. each raw and burnt sienna. The second color is 4oz. (120ml.) white latex flat, with ½tsp. each dioxazine purple and Payne's gray, while the third color is 4oz. (120ml.) white latex flat with 2tsp. raw umber.

Allow the second coat of colorwash to dry (4 hours).

3 Mask off the two remaining sections in a similar way allowing the new masking to overlap the adjoining sections, and not omitting the masking tape for the straight edge.

4 Mix the second and third colors in screw-top jars. Dilute a few tablespoons of each color with equal parts of glazing liquid and 4 parts water on plates. Using the same technique as in step 2, give two coats of colorwash to the top right-hand section with the diluted second color, and two to the bottom left-hand section with the diluted third color.

5 The top corners of the window are painted in the undiluted version of their colorwash. The torn-paper masks that are still in place will give soft edges. For their straight edges, use masking tape placed horizontally and vertically in line with the window opening. Use a small paintbrush to paint each corner. Remove all the masking.

6 At each place where the colors overlap at the sides and at the top, use four pieces of torn paper to mask off a loose diamond motif. Attach the pieces of torn paper to the wall with spray adhesive, and paint each of the diamonds in one of the three colors using a small paintbrush.

❷ GRAY, CAFÉ AU LAIT, AND AQUA OVER OFF-WHITE
This background is 17oz. (500ml.) white latex flat lightly tinted with 4tsp. neutral gray. The first color is 4oz. (120ml.) white latex flat with 1tsp. ultramarine and ½tsp. yellow ocher. The second color is 4oz. (120ml.) white latex flat mixed with 2tsp. each burnt sienna and Payne's gray, and the third color is 6tbsp. white latex flat, plus 2tbsp. ultramarine and 1tbsp. yellow ocher.

Window frame

Remove the masking from the window frame and use one of the 1in. (25mm.) paintbrushes to give the frame two coats of the second color, allowing 2–4 hours for each coat to dry.

155

SEASIDE DOORS

Even if you live far from the coast, this treatment for doors will give you an appetite for long summer days on the beach. More California than New England, more Mediterranean than British, the colors have been chosen to bring a sunny atmosphere into any interior. If you are anxious to create the look of real weatherbeaten beach-house doors, you will need thick base coats of latex flat to give you plenty of leeway when you are rubbing back. Over these we have stenciled a distant view of a boat in full sail, and a close-up of its striped flag. Keep the painting loose. It should look as if it had to be painted quickly. Vacations are not for work.

BASIC RECIPE—SAND ON SKY BLUE

PREPARATION

Prepare the surface thoroughly. See pages 26–9.

INGREDIENTS

For 2 standard cabinet doors
First base coat ▶ 10oz. (300ml.) white latex flat paint / 3tbsp. ultramarine artists' acrylic color
Second base coat ▶ 10oz. (300ml.) white latex flat paint / 3tbsp. yellow ocher artists' acrylic color
Sails, hull, and flag (colors not mixed together) ▶ 1tbsp. white artists' acrylic color / 1tbsp. ultramarine artists' acrylic color / scant ¼tsp. naphthol red artists' acrylic color

EQUIPMENT

2 screw-top jars / 2 x 3in. (75mm.) paintbrushes / fine-grit waterproof sand paper / 1 cellulose sponge and 3 pieces / rag / tracing paper / pencil / paper / repositionable spray adhesive / stencil board / X-Acto knife / cutting mat / ruler / water-soluble marker / 3 saucers / small artists' brush / masking tape

INSTRUCTIONS
Base coats

1 Since you will be applying thick coats of paint which are likely to run, remove your cabinet doors and work on them on a horizontal surface.
2 Mix each of the base-coat colors in the screw-top jars. You should have sufficient to apply two good thick coats of each color.
3 Fully load one of the paintbrushes with paint, and apply a generous layer of the first color. Do not worry about brush marks, but in fact aim to leave them showing. However, be organized in the order in which you paint. Start with the door panels, followed by the rails (horizontal), then the stiles (vertical). Finally, paint the edges. Always finish by brushing

out the paint in the same direction as the grain of the wood. Leave to dry. Latex flat paint can normally be re-coated after 4 hours, but the thicker coats used here may need to be left a little longer.

4 The doors will need a second coat of blue, applied in the same way, followed by two coats of yellow. After the final coat, leave to harden for a day.

5 To create the desired weatherbeaten look, sand the final yellow coat with the sand paper dipped in water (see pages 54–5). This not only leaves a flat, matte finish, but also breaks through the yellow to reveal the blue brush marks below. You can rub off extra yellow in those places where paint would have worn more quickly—for example, around handles and along edges. As you do this, a slurry of paint and water will form, which you should wipe off with a wet sponge as you proceed.

6 Once you are happy with the look of the doors, dry them off with a rag.

Boat motif

1 Trace the designs for the boat and the flag (see page 186), enlarge them on a photocopier, and use them to make the stencils (see page 30).

2 Using the ruler and the water-soluble marker, measure and mark the position of the boat in the center of the door panel. Position the boat stencil 1¼in. (3cm.) below and to the right of it as required for the shadow, then sponge the shadow in lightly, using 1tbsp. of the base coat yellow mixed on a saucer with a tiny amount of yellow ocher, just enough to take it down a tone.

3 The shadow will dry quickly, so within a few minutes you can reposition the stencil to paint in the boat itself. Sponge in the hull using the ultramarine blue spooned into a saucer.

4 Sponge the sails in white in the same way, then use the small artists' brush to add their red stripes.

Flag motif

1 For the striped flag, apply masking tape to leave a central rectangle. Its size will be governed by the size of your door panel. Sponge the rectangle in white.

2 Position the flag stencil—the wavy lines—over the white sponged rectangle, and sponge in the ultramarine. Remove the stencil and the masking tape and allow the paint to dry (1 hour).

3 For the shadow, apply masking tape inside the bottom and right-hand edges of the flag, with another line of tape about 1¼in. (3cm.) from the first, to create an L-shaped area.

❶ SAND ON SKY BLUE
The basic recipe.

❷ SKY BLUE ON SAND
If you prefer sky blues to golden sands, simply reverse the base coats. Everything else remains the same, except, of course, for the shadows, which you make by adding a smidgen of ultramarine to a tablespoon of the blue top coat.

Sponge this in, using the same yellow as you used for the boat's shadow. Both this shadow and that of the boat should give the impression of the boat and flag floating in front of the door on a sunny day.

4 If the boat and flag look a little too freshly painted, you can use the sand paper again with water to give them a worn and weatherbeaten look. But gently does it—the paint here is much thinner than the paint of the base coats, and if you are too vigorous as you sand, you will remove the boat and flag completely.

ROMAN-NUMERAL DOORS

Many of us have inherited kitchen cabinets with poor-quality or worn-looking doors. One alternative to replacing them is to repaint them. The doors on these pages have one of the most common shapes available. To decorate them, we have borrowed classical elements of ornamentation—the circle-within-a-square motif combined with a handwritten Roman numeral—but have painted them in modern colors. You may well find similar numerals or letters on an old document or, as we did, in a book of italic writing.

The wax-resist technique used to give some parts of these doors their aged look was also used for the numerals. The wax is easy to apply to the numerals, and lends itself well to rendering their soft, uneven handwritten edges. If you have several doors, consider numbering them in sequence. You could also use the design for matching kitchen drawer fronts, provided the drawers are deep enough. Otherwise, they would be best painted just with the background colors.

BASIC RECIPE—KHAKI OVER ULTRAMARINE

PREPARATION | **Prepare the surface thoroughly. See pages 26–9.**

INGREDIENTS | *For 4 standard kitchen cabinet doors*
First color ▶ 10tbsp. ultramarine artists' acrylic color / 5tbsp. white latex flat paint / 2½tsp. quinacridone violet artists' acrylic color
Resist ▶ 4tbsp. (approx.) beeswax
Second color ▶ 8½oz. (250ml.) white latex flat paint / 10tsp. yellow ocher artists' acrylic color / 1tsp. Payne's gray artists' acrylic color
First half-square motif ▶ 2tbsp. Mars red artists' acrylic color
Second half-square motif ▶ 2tbsp. first color
Circle motif ▶ 5tsp. ready-mixed black latex flat paint / 1½tsp. phthalocyanine blue artists' acrylic color / 1tsp. white latex flat paint
Protective coat ▶ 3½oz. (100ml.) beeswax or furniture polish

EQUIPMENT | **3 screw-top jars / 2 x 2in. (50mm.) paintbrushes / tracing paper / paper / chalk / hard pencil / jar / saucepan / small, old artists' brush / water-soluble marker / ruler / compass / 3 small flat artists' brushes / 3 medium flat artists' brushes / spatula / waterproof sand paper / bowl of water / lint-free cloth**

INSTRUCTIONS
Base coats
1 Mix the four colors in the screw-top jars.
2 Use one of the paintbrushes to apply two fairly thick layers of the first color to the door, allowing 4 hours for each coat of paint to dry.

ROMAN-NUMERAL DOORS

Resist

1 Enlarge a Roman numeral of your choice to suit the size of your door, then trace and transfer it to the upper section of the door panel, as shown here, using chalk, tracing paper, and a hard pencil.

2 Melt the beeswax (see page 75), and use the old artists' brush to fill in the Roman numerals with the melted wax. Do not use a good brush, as it becomes useless for painting once its bristles have wax on.

3 To give the door an aged look, use the same brush to apply a little wax to the edges of the moldings. The wax will set immediately.

4 Again use a paintbrush to apply two layers of the second color over the whole door, including the resist, in the same way as the first.

❶ KHAKI OVER ULTRAMARINE The basic recipe gives a set of colors that will harmonize well with a variety of color schemes. Note how the numeral has been left with a crisp finish in contrast to the lightly aged treatment of the moldings.

Motif

1 The size of the circle-in-a-square motif is governed by the dimensions of your door panel. Our motif measured 9 x 9in. (22.5 x 22.5cm.) and the circle had a diameter of 6in. (15cm.). Draw them beneath the numerals using a water-soluble marker, ruler, and a compass.

2 Use the artists' brushes and the appropriate colors to paint each section of the motif. These will also need two coats of paint, but acrylic paint dries quickly, so there will be no waiting time.

3 When the painting is complete, leave to dry for around an hour. The paint must not be too hard for the next stage.

4 Use the spatula to remove the wax, together with its coating of paint, scraping the spatula gently across the surface of the door. This will reveal the number, leaving it looking clean and neat. Enhance the aged look by lightly scraping the moldings and rubbing them with the sand paper dipped in water.

Protective coat

Finally, rub the whole door thoroughly with beeswax or furniture polish applied on a lint-free cloth. This will give it a natural-looking shine as well as a protective coating.

❷ YELLOW OCHER OVER EMERALD GREEN A brighter set of colors. The first coats are 10tbsp. white latex flat, 10tbsp. phthalocyanine green, and 2½tbsp. Payne's gray. After the resist is applied, it is painted over with 8½oz. (250ml.) yellow ocher. The square motif is painted half in green (2tbsp. of the first color), and half in a mixture of 1tbsp. each Mars red and dioxazine purple. The circle is in 8tsp. khaki, the second color from the basic recipe.

❸ BLUE BLACK OVER KHAKI A more dramatic way to revamp dingy kitchen cabinets. Start by applying two coats of the khaki second color from the basic recipe. Next, add 4tbsp. phthalocyanine blue and 7tsp. white artists' acrylic colors to 6½oz. (190ml.) black latex flat, apply the resist, and paint this mixture on top. The half-squares are in 2tbsp. khaki and 2tbsp. yellow ocher, and the circle is painted in blue – 7½tsp. of the basic recipe first color.

FURNITURE &
ACCESSORIES

Decorated furniture and accessories have recently been making a comeback. Having spent the last five decades blending into the background, cupboards, tables, chairs, lamps, lamp bases—almost any piece of household paraphernalia you can think of—are now flaunting painted motifs that can set the tone for a whole decorating scheme.

The history of applying painted design to furniture and accessories has a long pedigree, going back to ancient times and spanning the whole world. You need only think of the painted beds and chairs discovered in the tomb of Tutankhamun, or of the glowing lacquered paintwork of ancient Chinese screens and tables.

The French salons of the eighteenth century may be a little over the top for current taste, but there a painted object was certainly appreciated, be it a footstool, the latest writing desk, or a piano. Painting a piano is considered something close to a crime these days, but we wouldn't say no to the challenge. Nor did the artists Vanessa Bell and Duncan Grant, who in the early twentieth century, lived in and decorated almost every available surface of their extraordinary home at Charleston in Sussex, England. According to the artistic taste of their time, they appeared to be breaking new ground, but in fact they were simply following a tradition of folk art that has been around for centuries in places as far apart as Russia, Mexico, Sweden, New England, and Australia.

Painting your own furniture and accessories is not as daunting as it may appear, and hopefully the ideas on the following pages will be just

Right: A glimpse into a bathroom at Charleston confounds our expectations—it is the wall that has been left plain and the furniture that has been patterned. Mostly done freehand, this decoration could inspire you with the same freedom of spirit.

Below: These three cat lovers' seats have been decorated in naive style with the simplest of handpainted stripes. The technique is simple, but the overall effect is one of great subtlety.

what you need to inspire you. As with our other designs and projects, we have not used any arcane techniques or materials that are peculiar to the painting of furniture and accessories. In fact, the opposite is true. Everything you see here could be applied to any of the other surfaces you might care to decorate.

What you may find, though, is that working on a small area such as a picture frame or table top, can make you rather adventurous. Two of the three table tops in this section grew out of our own experimental work with stone effects. Starting with the idea of a limestone-looking surface and our fondness for spiral shapes, the addition of an ammonite to the limestone seemed an obvious choice, providing, we think, a happy combination of two very ancient forms. And the slate-effect table was the result of our seeing what would happen if we combined a slate finish with two of our most frequently used techniques—sponging a glaze on and sponging one off.

Once you have read this section of the book, we hope you will look around your home with new eyes, seeking out pieces of furniture or accessories that could benefit from a facelift. Often all that is needed is a fresh coat of paint and a small motif stenciled in one corner to give something a look that is bang up to date. Alternatively, buy or make something simple—a table needs only to be a piece of board on large casters—with the specific idea of adding your own personal touch. And if you don't like the result, you can always sand it off and try again.

Below: Contemporary decorated furniture and accessories which borrow freely from a variety of sources. The vibrant eclectic mix is linked together by a careful choice of coloring.

JAPANESE FABRIC
SCREEN

This project combines rugged builders' props with a light, translucent fabric. It would make an excellent solution to screening off an area of a room for those of you who do not wish to use more traditional screens. When choosing a site for your screen, make sure that the ceiling is solid enough to take the upward force of the props. If possible, locate the screen below a beam. There will be no need to over-tighten the props, as they will be supporting only the fabric, not the building.

BASIC RECIPE—RAW SIENNA AND NEUTRAL GRAY ON CREAM

PREPARATION

Prepare the surface thoroughly. See pages 26–9.

INGREDIENTS

For a screen 6½ x 4½ft. (2 x 1.4m.)
Screen ▶ 6½ x 5ft. (2 x 1.5m) dark cream roller-shade fabric / 13ft. (4m.) double-sided transparent tape / 7ft. x ½in. (2.2m. x 12mm.) diameter metal rod / 6½ft. x ½in. (2m. x 12mm.) diameter metal rod / 2 adjustable builders' props to suit your room size
First color ▶ 2tbsp. raw sienna artists' acrylic color
Second color ▶ 2tbsp. neutral gray artists' acrylic color
Lines ▶ 2tbsp. white artists' acrylic color
Optional ▶ aerosol can silver paint

EQUIPMENT

2 large pieces stencil board / 1in. (25mm.) wide (minimum) masking tape / straightedge / pencil / 20in. (50cm.) string plus pin / scissors / tape measure / repositionable spray adhesive / 3 large pieces cellulose sponge / 3 saucers / paper / scraps of padding (see Notes)

INSTRUCTIONS
Stencil

1 The design is made up of three large motifs, each stenciled using the same 24in. (60cm.) diameter stencil. Since stencil board rarely comes this big, you will have to join two pieces of board together. To do this, lay the two pieces flat on a table or on the floor with their edges butting up to one another, then stick masking tape down the join on both faces of the board.

2 Use the straightedge and a pencil to mark the diagonals of the board; to draw the circle, pin the end of the string at the center of the board where the diagonals cross. Pull the string

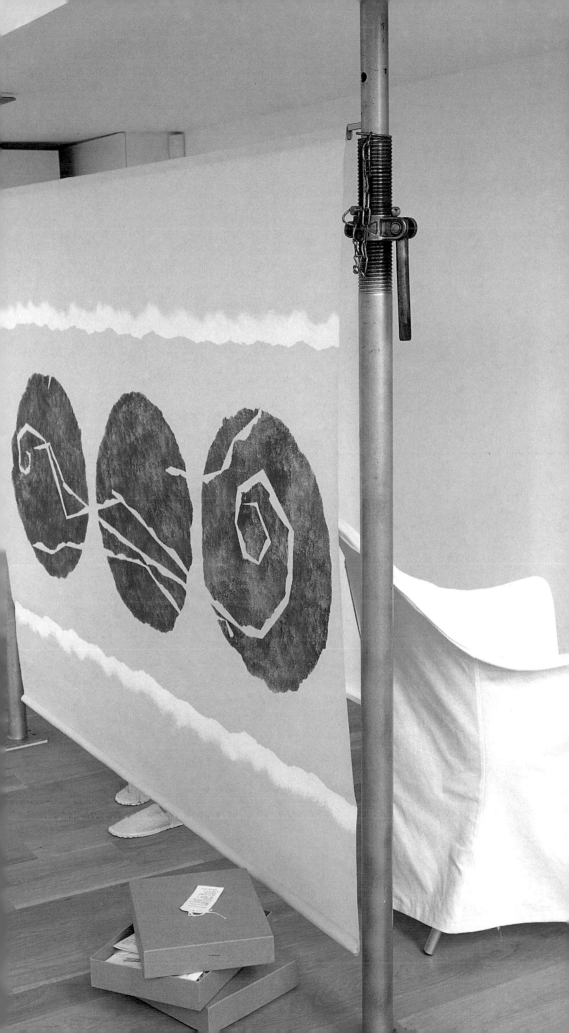

tight, and attach the pencil 12in. (30cm.) from the pin using masking tape. Place the pencil point on the card and sweep it around the pin, keeping the string taut. Do not worry if the circle you end up with is less than perfect.

3 Make a hole in the stencil board with the scissors, then carefully tear the board along the line you have drawn to remove the circle.

Motifs

1 Lay the shade material out on a flat surface. Use the floor if you do not have a table large enough. The motifs are stenciled horizontally across the center of the material, with 2in. (5cm.) spaces between. Measure out and mark for the positioning of the motifs using small pieces of masking tape. Do not use pencil or marker, as these marks will be difficult to remove from the fabric.

2 Spray the back of the stencil with adhesive and place it in its first position.

3 To make the lines that run through the circles, firmly stick small strips of masking tape torn along their length to the fabric framed by the stencil. Build up the design following the examples shown here.

4 Trim two of the pieces of cellulose sponge into balls using scissors. Spoon a little of each of the first and second colors into separate saucers, and use the rounded pieces of sponge to apply them to the fabric. The textured effect is created by sponging on the two colors at the same time and letting them overlap in places. There is no need to blend them into one another.

5 Remove the masking tape and the stencil, and allow to dry (20 minutes).

6 Repeat, placing the stencil in its second and third positions. For each new motif, use fresh masking tape positioned so as to continue the linear element of the design.

Lines

1 A sponged white line runs 6in. (15cm) above and below the row of circles. The inner edge of each of these lines is masked off with segments of torn paper (see page 36). The outer edge is faded off with the sponge. Use a long straightedge laid on the fabric as a guide to positioning the first torn-paper mask. Spoon some of the white paint into

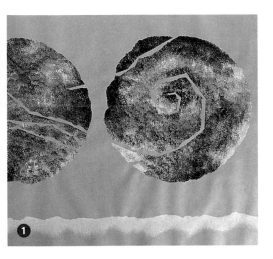

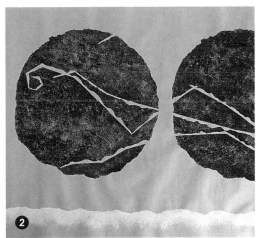

another saucer, and use a sponge to apply it along this edge, fading the color away to make a line approximately 2in. (5cm.) wide. You are not aiming for a line of a perfectly constant width. Remove the masking paper and allow to dry (20 minutes).

2 Repeat for the second line, allowing 1 hour to dry.

Making the screen

1 Turn the stenciled fabric over and stick half the double-sided tape to the top edge. Lay the longer rod on the tape, leaving 4in. (10cm.) protruding at each end. Roll the fabric over and around the rod, fixing it in place with the tape.

2 Repeat, using the shorter rod for the lower edge of the stenciled fabric.

3 If you feel, as we did, that the adjustable props need smartening up, spray them with the spray paint, following the manufacturers' instructions.

4 Now you will need some help. Adjust the props to the height of your room and set one prop in position, making sure that the holes in its inner sliding section face inward. Slot the longer rod of the screen into one of these holes at the desired height, making sure that the screen is facing the right way around.

5 Move the second prop into place, pushing it along the floor until the rod slides into the corresponding hole on this prop. Fix the second prop in position, and your screen is finished and in place.

Notes Builders' props are not the most delicate of objects and can leave marks on your floor and ceiling. Prevent this by using padding. Scraps of foam rubber, cork, or carpet would all be suitable.

❶ ACHROMATIC The first color uses 2tbsp. Payne's gray and the second 2tbsp. white, in addition to the 2tbsp. white for the two lines.

❷ COBALT BLUE AND TERRA COTTA The first color is 2tbsp. cobalt blue, and the second is 2tbsp. Mars red. The white lines are as in the basic recipe. This recipe gives a more colorful version.

MOCK-SLATE
COFFEE TABLE

Slate slabs look wonderful but would be too heavy for a table that is sometimes moved around. They are also expensive. Our alternative—mock slate produced with artists' acrylic color that is burnished as it dries—overcomes both these problems. We took the opportunity to combine it with a painted design. For our basic recipe, we applied it in a deep sea blue to a wooden surface, but there is no reason why it could not be applied in other colors to other surfaces—garden pots for example or stenciled motifs on a sunroom wall.

BASIC RECIPE—DEEP SEA-BLUE AND SLATE GRAY

PREPARATION   **Prepare the surface thoroughly. See pages 26–9.**

INGREDIENTS   *For a coffee table*
Base coat ▶ 3½oz. (100ml.) white latex flat paint
First glaze coat ▶ 2tbsp. Payne's gray artists' acrylic color
Second glaze coat ▶ 1tsp. phthalocyanine blue artists' acrylic color / 1tsp. phthalocyanine green artists' acrylic color
Slate undercoat ▶ 3½oz. (100ml.) black latex flat paint
Slate topcoat ▶ 5tbsp. Payne's gray artists' acrylic color / 1tbsp. white artists' acrylic color / 1tbsp. phthalocyanine green artists' acrylic color / 2tsp. burnt umber artists' acrylic color
Lines ▶ 1tsp. neutral gray artists' acrylic color / ½tsp. Mars black artists' acrylic color
Burnishing ▶ small can of furniture wax or beeswax
Protective coat ▶ 1–2tbsp. furniture wax

EQUIPMENT   **Small, smooth paint roller plus tray / fine-grit sandpaper / tape measure / water-soluble marker / 2 saucers / 3 cellulose sponges / bowl of water / 3 screw-top jars / paper / repositionable spray adhesive / 1 x 2in. (50mm.) paintbrush / flexible spatula / medium flat artists' brush / lint-free cloth**

INSTRUCTIONS   Use the smooth roller to paint the whole table top with the
Base coat   latex flat paint. This will leave a fine, smooth texture. Allow to dry (4 hours), then sand lightly.

Cross   Our table measures 48 x 18in. (120 x 45cm.). The long arm of the cross on it is 2½in. (6cm.) wide, and the short arm is 5½in. (14cm.) wide. The dimensions of yours will depend on the size of your table. Using a tape measure and the water-soluble marker, roughly sketch out the cross, drawing it 2in. (5cm.) larger all around than the finished design. Do not forget to extend the arms of the cross over the edges of the table as we did.

Glaze coats

1 Spoon a little of the first glaze coat into a saucer, and sponge it loosely into the cross. There is no need to attempt to sponge a neat edge, as this will be created at a later stage. Before the paint dries, splash and flick water onto it, then sponge off with a clean, damp sponge to leave a variegated texture (see pages 51–2). Allow to dry (1 hour).

2 Mix the second glaze coat in a small screw-top jar, and spoon a little into a saucer. With a clean, barely damp sponge, rub a transparent layer of this color over the first. Allow to harden (1 hour).

Masking

1 Again using the water-soluble marker, lightly redraw the cross, this time to the exact dimensions. Mask off the cross using torn paper held in place with spray adhesive (see page 79). If you tear the paper along its grain, it will give the cross its straight, soft edges. Again, remember to extend the arms of the cross over the edges of the table.

2 With the paintbrush and the slate undercoat, paint in the four exposed rectangles of the table top. Allow the paint to dry (4 hours).

Burnishing

1 Mix together the colors for the slate topcoat in another screw-top jar. Use the spatula to apply this mixture to a small area of a painted rectangle. Create the polished-slate look by

burnishing the paint. To achieve this, use small, circular movements of the spatula while the paint dries. As the paint becomes tacky, add a little wax to the surface and continue burnishing. The wax makes it easier to manipulate the spatula and also forms part of the hard, polished, slate-like finish as it is driven into the paint. Add more wax as and when you need it.

With practice, you will be able to judge when the paint is dry enough for burnishing, as well as what slight changes can be achieved in the patina by variations in the timing, waxing, and burnishing.

Work across the surface of the table in this way and don't stop until you

MOCK-SLATE COFFEE TABLE

DEEP SEA BLUE AND SLATE GRAY
The basic recipe.

VENETIAN RED AND SLATE GRAY
Here, the base coat, the first glaze coat, and the slate undercoat and topcoat are as in the basic recipe. The second glaze coat is 2tsp. magenta and 1tsp. burnt sienna, while the lines are painted using 1½tsp. neutral gray.

DARK YELLOW AND SLATE GRAY
Again, the base coat, the first glaze coat, and the slate undercoat and topcoat are as in the basic recipe. The second glaze coat uses 2tsp. Hansa yellow light and ¼tsp. neutral gray, and the lines are painted using a mixture of 1tsp. neutral gray and ¼tsp. white.

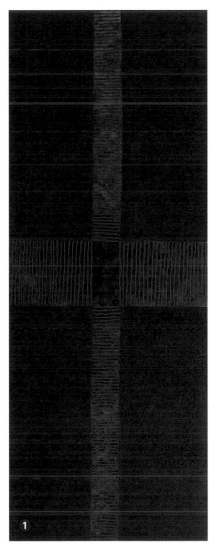

1

2

3

have completed a whole rectangle. Treat the edges of the table in the same way. The whole procedure will take some time, but it is not arduous and there is great satisfaction to be gained from watching the texture surface form beneath the spatula as you work.

2 Remove all the paper masking and leave the paint to harden thoroughly overnight.

Lines

Mix the color for the lines in another screw-top jar and use the artists' brush to paint them across the arms of the cross. Twist the brush a little as you paint in order to create variations in their width. Note that the central section of the table does not have any lines. Allow to dry for a day.

Protective coat

Use a soft, lint-free cloth to wax the whole table.

171

CHECKERBOARD
TABLE TOPS

Table tops—provided they are finished with a protective coat to stop them from getting damaged during use—are the ideal surface for many of the decorative paint techniques we use in this book. These checkerboard table tops are another example of what can be achieved. If we had painted a regular checkerboard pattern on them, they could have been used for playing checkers, but we decided to throw in an asymmetric section, which varies from table to table. You will find that the squares-within-squares are easy to mark out and apply. You will also be able to adapt them to suit any size table. And if you do not have a table, then just paint a board of the size you want, and set it on the biggest wheels you can find.

BASIC RECIPE—SAGE ON RED

PREPARATION

Prepare the surface thoroughly. See pages 26–9.

INGREDIENTS

For a small side table
Base coat ▶ 6tbsp. white latex flat paint
First glaze coat ▶ 2tbsp. Payne's gray artists' acrylic color
Second glaze coat ▶ 1tbsp. magenta artists' acrylic color / ½tbsp. alizarin crimson artists' acrylic color
Green checks ▶ 4tsp. white artists' acrylic color / 1tsp. phthalocyanine green artists' acrylic color / 1½tsp. Payne's gray artists' acrylic color / 2tsp. raw umber artists' acrylic color
Beige checks ▶ 2tsp. white artists' acrylic color / ¼tsp. raw umber artists' acrylic color
Gray checks ▶ 2tsp. Payne's gray artists' acrylic color
Protective coat ▶ 3tbsp. flat or satin acrylic varnish

EQUIPMENT

1 x 3in. (75mm.) paintbrush / fine-grit sand-paper / 4 saucers / 4 cellulose sponges / bowl of water / 2 screw-top jars / ruler / water-soluble marker / 2 x ⅜in. (10mm.) flat artists' brushes / 1 x 2in. (50mm.) varnish brush

CHECKERBOARD TABLE TOPS

INSTRUCTIONS
Base coats

Using the ordinary paintbrush, apply two coats of white latex flat, allowing 4 hours for each coat to dry. Sand down lightly between coats and after the last coat has dried, to remove any bits of hardened paint or dust; otherwise they may show up later as white spots in the finished surface.

Glaze coats

1 Spoon the Payne's gray into a saucer and sponge it loosely onto the table top and sides (see page 50).

2 Immediately splash the surface with water, then use a clean sponge to sponge off some of the gray paint, leaving a heavily variegated texture (see pages 51–2). Allow the paint to dry (1 hour).

3 Mix together the magenta and alizarin crimson in a saucer. Dip a clean, damp sponge into this mix and rub it into the surface, leaving a transparent coating over the gray. Your table top should now look like an exotic piece of polished marble. Allow to dry (1 hour).

Painting the
checks

1 Meanwhile, mix the colors for the checks.

2 Mark a checkerboard grid on the table top, using the marker. Aim for squares with sides of approximately 2in. (5cm.). Each of our designs is different, although all are based on a common grid. In this example, a group of twenty-one squares has been subdivided into smaller squares.

3 Using the artists' brushes, paint the squares, the alternate larger ones in green and the smaller ones in beige and

Payne's gray. Spoon a small amount of each color into a saucer, and load your brushes from there. If the paint does not flow smoothly, you may need to add a little water.

4 As you complete every two or three squares and before they dry, flick or splash a little water over them, as you did earlier. Leave for a moment, then press a clean, damp sponge onto the squares to create the texture seen in the example. Don't forget to paint the edges.

5 Set your table aside for a couple of days after finishing it to allow the paint to really harden off. Using the varnish brush, apply a minimum of two coats of varnish according to the manufacturers' instructions.

❶ SAGE ON RED
The basic recipe.

❷ DUSTY MAUVE ON EMERALD
Our second table top, which is predominantly green, is started in the same manner as the first. The first glaze coat is 2tbsp. Payne's gray. Two glaze coats of phthalo-cyanine green, a total of 2tbsp., are rubbed into it to make quite a dark tone. The larger checks are painted in a mixture of 4tsp. white, 2tsp. ultramarine, 1tsp. Payne's gray, and ½tsp. magenta. The subdivided checks are painted with 2tsp. Mars red and 2tsp. Payne's gray.

❸ DUSTY MAUVE ON LIME
The thIrd table top begins again with a sponged-on base coat of white latex flat, followed by a glaze coat of 2tbsp. Payne's gray. A thin glaze of 1tbsp. Hansa yellow light is rubbed into that. This gives a lovely depth to the painted surface, reminiscent of marble, though it must be said it is not a marble you are likely to find in a quarry. In this design, a line of larger checks has been added, crossing from one side to the other. The blue checks are in the same blue as the checks in recipe 2, while the green checks are in 2tsp. green from the basic recipe, and the red checks are painted using 2tsp. Mars red.

COLORED & COMBED
PICTURE FRAMES

These frames are designed to be at least as attractive as their contents. If you do not have any pictures that can stand up to a blaze of color around them, use the frames to surround beachcombings or any other found objects which you find attractive enough to warrant a place on your wall. Alternatively, they would make vibrant and unusual frames for mirrors.

Choose a frame to decorate that has as wide and flat a face as possible to allow for the design to be applied with a comb. This tool is really for imitation wood-graining, but the ridges of paint it leaves behind can be decorative in themselves. The effect is not dissimilar to the look of tapestry, although the colors here are far removed from the traditional colors of tapestry. The woven effect can be enhanced by allowing the occasional curve and wiggle to occur as you pull the comb along, and by varying the pressure here and there to reveal differing amounts of the base coat. For our frames, the combing is not the final coat—it has been painted over with stripes and then rubbed back to reveal some of the combing color beneath.

BASIC RECIPE—VIBRANT RED AND GREENS

PREPARATION	**Prepare the surface thoroughly. See pages 26–9.**
INGREDIENTS	*For a frame 24 x 16in. (60 x 40cm.)* Base coat ▸ 4tbsp. naphthol red artists' acrylic color Combing color ▸ 2tbsp. white artists' acrylic color / 2tbsp. phthalocyanine green artists' acrylic color Stripe color ▸ 4tbsp. white artists' acrylic color / ½tsp. phthalocyanine green artists' acrylic color
EQUIPMENT	**3 screw-top jars / 2 x 2in. (50mm.) paintbrushes / safe-release masking tape / tape measure / 1 x 3in. (75mm.) fine decorators' comb / 2 or 3 cellulose sponges / 1 x ¼in. (6mm.) flat artists' brush / fine-grit waterproof sand paper / bowl of water**
INSTRUCTIONS **Base coats**	Mix the three colors in the screw-top jars. Use an ordinary paintbrush to apply two coats of the base color to the frame, ensuring that the inner and outer edges are painted. Leave 2–4 hours between coats.
Combing	**1** Use masking tape to mask off ⅜in. (1cm.) of the inner edges of two opposite sides of your frame. Also mask the diagonals to create the miters. **2** Since acrylic paint dries quickly, you should now proceed

without too many pauses. Use a paintbrush to apply the combing color fairly generously along one side of the frame, then immediately run the comb firmly down the full length (see pages 60–61). Once you are happy with the result—if you do not like it, you can immediately wipe it off with a wet sponge and start again—repeat on the opposite side. Leave the combing to dry for about 1 hour, then repeat for the other two sides. Take care when using the masking tape on freshly painted surfaces.

Stripes

1 Now use masking tape to mask off about ⅜in. (1cm.) of the outer edges of two opposite sides of your frame, as well as the two miters.

2 Using the stripe color and the flat artists' brush, paint in

COLORED AND COMBED PICTURE FRAMES

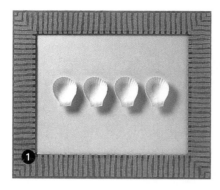

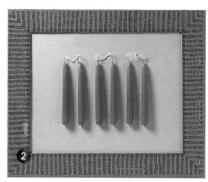

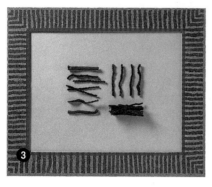

❷ VIOLET, GRAY, AND GINGER
These colors consist of a base coat of 2tbsp. white mixed with 4tsp. magenta and a touch of Payne's gray. The combing is done using 10tsp. white mixed with 3tsp. phthalo-cyanine green and 1tsp. naphthol red. The stripes are 4tbsp. Mars red.

❸ FLAME, AZURE, AND TAUPE
These colors consist of a base coat of 10tsp. Hansa yellow light, mixed with 2tsp. naphthol red. The combing is done with 4tbsp. white mixed with ½tsp. phthalocyanine blue, and the stripes are 2tbsp. white with 1tbsp. Mars red, 1½tsp. phthalocyanine green, and ½tsp. naphthol red.

❹ CITRON, VIOLET, AND GRAY
These colors consist of a base coat of 2tbsp. Hansa yellow light combed with a mixture of 11tbsp. white, 4tsp. magenta, and a touch of Payne's gray. The stripes are painted with 10tsp. white mixed with 1tbsp. phthalo-cyanine green and 1tsp. naphthol red.

❶ VIBRANT RED AND GREENS
The basic recipe.

the stripes in a loose freehand. It does not matter if they are slightly unevenly spaced, as that is part of their charm. However, if you feel unsure about freehand painting, you can measure out the stripes and mark their positions on the masking tape. Leave the lines to dry for about 1 hour, then remove the masking tape.

3 Repeat for the final two sides, but omit the masking tape along the miters so that you can see the corner detail and join up the stripes as they meet. Leave to dry overnight.

Rubbing back

Armed with a bowl of water, a sponge, and the sand paper, you can now start to rub back the paint (see pages 54–5). As you do so, the combed color will be revealed as lines across the stripes, and the whole surface will be rubbed gently smooth. Avoid rubbing the edges of the frame unless you want an aged look. Once you have the result you want, give the whole frame a good wipe with a sponge and clean water, leave to dry, and it is ready for use.

Notes Slowpokes could use artists' oil colors instead of acrylics. These will give you more time to work, especially if your frame is very large or you are combing something big, such as a door. The downside of using oil paint is the long drying time between coats, not to mention the smell.

FOSSIL TABLE TOP

This design idea takes the stone-finish technique of pages 64–5 a step further, by setting an authentic-looking fossil ammonite into a stone-finished table top. Fossils are most commonly found in limestones. The limestones vary so much in color and texture that there is bound to be one that you like. We mimic one that leans toward pink, and another that leans toward yellow. The third is more granite than limestone, but you can be more fanciful with your coloring if you wish.

Fossils are beautiful but delicate and fragile. The use of thick paint over a whiting resist can readily create an effect that mimics their appearance. Be confident in the handling of your brush and in the application of the paint, and do not worry about drips or splashes, or misplaced resist. Anything can have happened to the fossil during the last 250 million years. And if you want to make your fossil bigger, then go ahead. They could grow to over six feet across.

BASIC RECIPE—PINK-TINTED LIMESTONE

PREPARATION

Prepare the surface thoroughly. See pages 26–9.

INGREDIENTS

For a small table
Base color ► 6tbsp. white latex flat paint / 1tsp. raw sienna artists' acrylic color
Resist ► 10tsp. whiting / 5tsp. water / ½tsp. wallpaper paste
First glaze coat ► 6tbsp. white latex flat paint / 5tsp. raw sienna artists' acrylic color / denatured alcohol
Second glaze coat ► 6tbsp. white latex flat paint / 2tsp. raw sienna artists' acrylic color / 2tsp. raw umber artists' acrylic color / denatured alcohol
Dabs ► scant ¼tsp. each Mars red, yellow ocher, and raw umber artists' acrylic colors
Protective coat ► 1tbsp. wax polish

EQUIPMENT

3 containers / coarse-textured paint roller plus tray / tracing paper / paper / hard pencil / chalk / screw-top jar / 1 x ¼in. (6mm.) artists' brush / repositionable spray adhesive / stencil board / X-Acto knife / cutting mat / 1 x 1in. (25mm.) old, stiff paintbrush / spatula / 3 cellulose sponges and 6 pieces / bowl of water / spray bottle / fine-grit waterproof sand paper / soft cloth

INSTRUCTIONS
Base coats

1 Mix the base color in one of the containers. Use the roller to apply two coats to the table top and its edges, allowing 2–4 hours for each coat to dry.

2 Trace the ammonite design from page 186, enlarge it on a photocopier to fit your table, then trace it onto the table top, using tracing paper, a hard pencil, and chalk.

FOSSIL TABLE TOP

❶ PINK-TINTED LIMESTONE
The basic recipe gives a pinkish limestone. We have been quite free with the addition of the dabs of color, especially the Mars red. The position of the ammonite on the table top is, of course, a matter of personal preference. Here we have placed i in one corner.

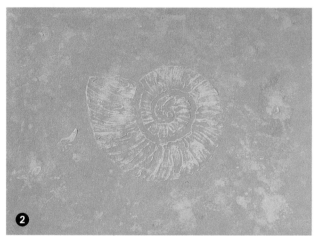

❷ YELLOW-TINTED LIMESTONE
Here we positioned the ammonite in the middle of the table and used a base coat of 6tbsp. white latex flat mixed with ½tsp. yellow ocher and ½tsp. raw umber, a first glaze of 6tbsp. white latex flat with 1tsp. raw umber and 2tsp. yellow ocher, and dabs of yellow ocher, white, and medium-gray. The second glaze was made from 6tbsp. white latex flat with 2tsp. neutral gray and ½tsp. yellow ocher, plus colored dabs.

❸ GRANITE
This swatch is based on the granite colors on page 64, but uses stronger colors and a more vigorous method to create this highly textured finish. The base coat is made of 6tbsp. white latex flat with 2tsp. neutral gray. The first glaze is 2tbsp. white latex flat with 4tbsp. Payne's gray and 4tsp. burnt umber. The second glaze consists of 1tbsp. white artists' acrylic color, dabbed and spread for a misty effect.

Resist
Mix the whiting, water, and wallpaper paste in a screw-top jar to make the resist (see pages 56-7). Use the round artists' brush to loosely paint the resist onto the sections left white on the design you have copied. Apply it quite thickly, and do not worry about being neat. Leave to dry for a few hours.

Stencil

1 Meanwhile, use your traced design to make a stencil of the ammonite outline (see page 30). Position the stencil on the table top over the ammonite, holding it in place with spray adhesive.

2 Using the old paintbrush, apply a thick layer of the base coat into the stencil and over the resist. In order to mimic the texture and pattern of the ammonite, brush the paint out so that it makes curved ridges running from the inner edge of the spiral to the outer edge. An old stiff brush is better for applying this layer than a new one, as an old one leaves good brush marks. If the brush marks disappear, allow to dry for a few moments, then repeat the process. Remove the stencil with care.

3 Spatter a few flicks of the base coat across the table top at random if you want more texture. Allow to harden for at least 4 hours, though it may take longer than usual since the paint has been applied so thickly.

4 Use the spatula and a damp sponge to gently remove the dried whiting resist, together with its covering of paint. This will reveal the ammonite, convincingly textured, but as yet without color.

Stone finish glazes

1 Mix the latex paint and raw sienna in a container to make the first glaze coat, and the latex paint, raw sienna, and raw umber in another container to make the second glaze coat. Complete the stone finish with these glaze coats, following the instructions on pages 64–5. Apply each glaze with a sponge across the whole of the table top, including the ammonite, as well as over the edges of the table. Sponge or splash with water, spray with denatured alcohol, and apply sponged-on dabs of Mars red, yellow ocher, and raw umber as desired. Aim for an open texture with plenty of variation. Take care not be too heavy-handed. You should try to achieve a subtle effect.

2 The ammonite will by now be almost camouflaged. To reveal it, very carefully sand away some of the two glazes from the ridges, using the sand paper dipped in water. This will give a worn look. You can accentuate the three-dimensional qualities by rubbing away a little more from one side of the spiral than from the other. However, care is called for, as the glaze coats are quite thin. You should also guard against rubbing away at other parts of the table top.

Protective coat

Leave aside for 24 hours, then buff up the whole of the table top with wax polish applied on a soft cloth.

MOTIFS & TEMPLATES

Most of the motifs we have used in our designs have been drawn here for you to trace. Many of them will have to be enlarged to the size you would like them, but this can easily be done on a photocopier. Note that some include registration marks, which must not be omitted when tracing or enlarging, as they are essential to the correct placement of the motif in a design.

Pages 48–9: Rubbing off

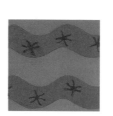

Pages 62–3: Stucco and embossing

Pages 66–7: Painting on glass

Pages 69–70: Overlapping stencils

Pages 73–4: An ornate stamp

Page 75: Painted wax resist

Page 78: Broken column border

Pages 92–5: Stamped squiggles on stripes

Pages 96–9: Late-summer seedhead frieze

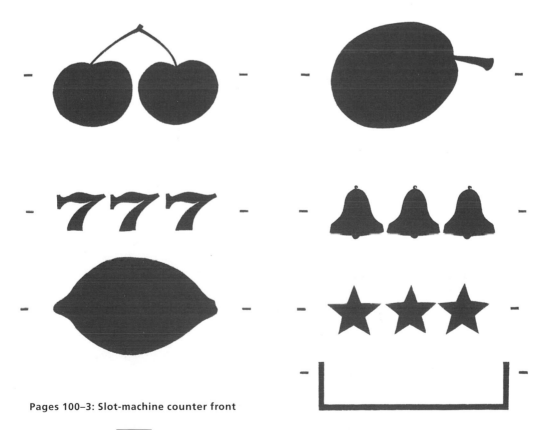

Pages 100–3: Slot-machine counter front

MOTIFS & TEMPLATES

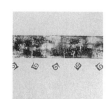

Pages 106–7: Oak-leaf border

Pages 111–13: Stipple and stucco

Pages 108–9: A simple border

Pages 116–19: Daisy-strewn floorboards

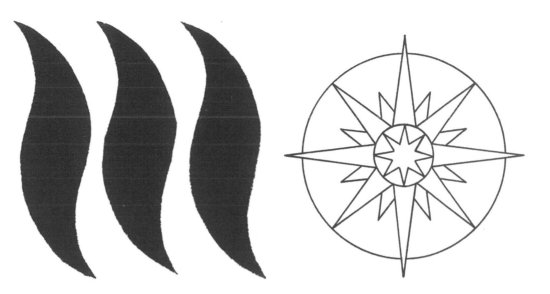

Pages 120–23: Kimonos on a concrete floor

Pages 128–9: Rose des Vents

Pages 140–43: Seaweed and shell closet

MOTIFS & TEMPLATES

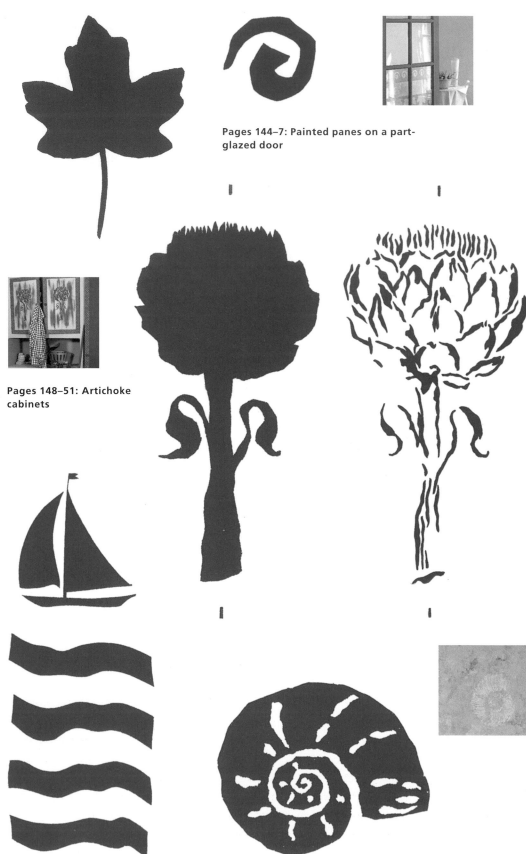

Pages 144–7: Painted panes on a part-glazed door

Pages 148–51: Artichoke cabinets

Pages 156–8: Seaside doors

Pages 179–81: Fossil table top

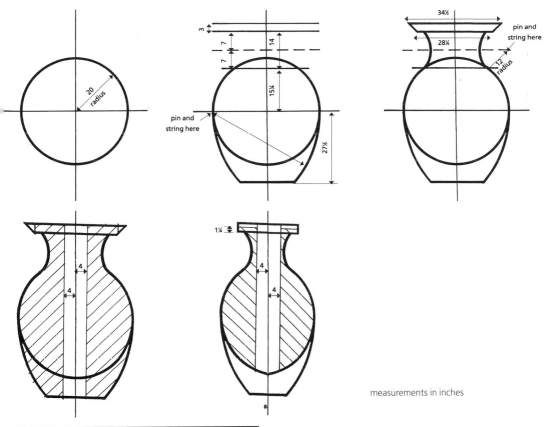

measurements in inches

TO MAKE THE VASE TEMPLATES

1 Cut lining wallpaper, or stiff brown paper, into two equal lengths and join together with masking tape to make a sheet 6ft. 6in. x 5ft. 2in. (2 x 1.6m.). Rule a vertical and a horizontal line midway along each side of the sheet. At the point where they cross—the sheet's center point—attach a piece of string with a pencil attached to it, and draw a circle with a radius of 20in. (50cm.).

2 Draw a horizontal line 27½in. (70cm.) below the first horizontal. Pin a string at the point where the circle crosses the first horizontal, stretch the string across to the other side of the circle, and anchor a pencil to the string at this point. Sweep the pencil downward, drawing an arc that meets the lower horizontal. Repeat on the other side. Draw three more horizontal lines above the first one, as shown in the diagram. Midway between the first and second of these three, draw a dotted horizontal line as shown.

3 Measure and mark along the dotted line 22in. (55cm.) on each side of the vertical. Attach a 12in. (30cm.) string and pencil at each of these two points in turn, and draw an arc. Following the diagram, measure 28¼in. (72cm.) and 35in. (88cm.) along the top two horizontals and join them as shown to make the rim of the vase. Cut this shape out to make the first template.

4 To make the second template, remove 8in. (20cm.) from the first template (unshaded areas), and cut the rim square. Rejoin the two parts with masking tape.

5 To make the third template, remove a further 8in. (20cm.) from the second template, reduce the depth of the rim by half, and cut away the lower part of the vase (unshaded areas). Rejoin the two parts with masking tape.

LIST OF SUPPLIERS

Most of the materials and equipment described in this book can be found in art supply stores and hardware/D.I.Y. stores. If you have difficulty finding any of the more specialized brushes and materials, consult the list below. A number of the companies listed here offer a mail-order sevice. However, bear in mind that some suppliers will not send toxic or flammable materials by mail.

✉ indicates that a mail-order/shipping service is available.

3M
ph: 800 722 5463
Call this number for your local supplier of Fineline tape

Arch ✉
407 Jackson Street
San Francisco, CA 94111
ph: 415 433 2724
Art supplies

The Art Store ✉
7301 West Beverly Boulevard
Los Angeles, CA 90036
ph: 213 933 9284 fx: 213 933 9794
Art supplies

Barclay Leaf Imports, Inc. ✉
21 Wilson Terrace
Elizabeth, NJ 07208
ph: 908 353 5522 fx: 908 353 5525
Gold leaf and gilding supplies

Bay City Paint Company ✉
2279 Market Street
San Francisco, CA 94114
ph: 415 431 4914
Specialty decorating supplies

Carter Sexton ✉
5308 Laurel Canyon Boulevard
North Hollywood, CA 91607
ph: 818 763 5050 fx: 818 763 1034
Art supplies

Charrette Favor Ruhl ✉
main location with other locations
throughout the Northeast
31 Olympia Avenue
Woburn, MA 01888
ph: 800 367 3729 fx: 800 626 7889
Art supplies

Curry's Art Supplies ✉
755 The Queensway E.
Mississauga, Ontario
L4Y 4C5
ph: (905) 272 4460
7 retail locations in Toronto; artist, craft, graphic design supplies and equipment

Easy Leaf Products ✉
6001 Santa Monica Boulevard
Los Angeles, CA 90038
ph: 213 469 0856 fx: 213 469 0940
Gold and other metal leaf

Guiry's, Inc. ✉
2468 South Colorado Boulevard
Denver, CO 80222
ph: 303 758 8244 fx: 303 756 3545
Art supplies

Janovic/Plaza Inc. ✉
30-35 Thomson Avenue
Long Island City, NY 11101
ph: 800 772 4381 fx: 718 361 7288
Specialty decorating supplies

Johnson Paint Co., Inc. ✉
355 Newbury Street
Boston, MA 02115
ph: 617 536 4838/4244
fx: 617 536 8832
Specialty decorating supplies, including imported brushes

Liberon/Star Supplies ✉
P.O. Box 86
Mendocino, CA 95460
ph: 800 245 5611 fx: 707 877 3566
Specialty decorating supplies including cold-patination fluid

Loew-Cornell, Inc. ✉
563 Chestnut Avenue
Teaneck, NJ 07666
ph: 201 836 7070 fx: 201 836 8110
Imported brushes and accessories

Pearl Paint Co., Inc. ✉
308 Canal Street
New York, NY 10013-2572
ph: 212 431 7932
Art supplies, including imported brushes

Progress Paint, KCI ✉
201 East Market Street
Louisville, KY 40202
ph: 502 584 0151
Specialty decorating supplies

Reed's Gold Leaf ✉
P.O. Box 160146
Nashville, TN 37216
ph: 615 865 2666 fx: 615 865 1903
Gilding supplies, manuals, and videos

Sam Flex Art Supplies ✉
main New York Store:
12 West 20th Street
New York, NY 10011
ph: 212 620 3038

also stores in:
Atlanta, GA ph: 404 352 7200
Orlando, FL ph: 407 898 9785
Art supplies

Texas Art Supply ✉
2001 Montrose Boulevard
Houston, TX 77006
ph: 713 526 5221 fx: 713 526 4062
Art supplies

TABLE OF EQUIVALENTS

Both standard and metric measurements are used in this book. Because some equivalents have been rounded up or down for convenience in measuring, it is important to choose either one system or the other and stick to it throughout that recipe.
   In following the recipes you may also find the following information useful.

1 cup	=	8 fl. oz.	=	16 tbsp.	=	240 ml.
½ cup	=	4 fl. oz.	=	8 tbsp.	=	120 ml.
¼ cup	=	2 fl. oz.	=	4 tbsp.	=	60 ml.
⅓ cup	=	2⅔ fl. oz.	=	5⅓ tbsp.	=	80 ml.
1 tbsp.	=	½ fl. oz.	=	3 tsp.	=	15 ml.
½ tbsp.	=	¼ fl. oz.	=	1½ tbsp.	=	7.5 ml.
1 tsp.	=	⅙ fl. oz.	=	⅓ tbsp.	=	5 ml.

INDEX

INDEX

ACKNOWLEDGMENTS

AUTHOR'S ACKNOWLEDGMENTS

Many people were involved in the making of this book, above all, Mary Evans and Jane O'Shea at Quadrille, and Hilary Mandleberg our editor, who have unfailingly encouraged and guided us throughout. All our projects have been enhanced by the photographers Debbie Patterson and Nicki Dowey, and by the designer Simon Balley. Priceless help with the projects was cheerfully given by Anice Bazoge and Diane Crawford, for whom simple thanks are not enough, while Jules Grant's timely arrival with a computer made the writing possible. A special thanks also goes to our student Melina Pachys, who gave up so much of her time to work on the projects with us. We are also grateful to Anice, Mary and Bruce, as well as to Jean-Claude and Fan, for giving up their walls and floors for our benefit. Lastly, thanks to Eleanor van Zandt and Maggi Mc Cormick for their invaluable help with the preparation of this American edition.

PICTURE ACKNOWLEDGMENTS

The publisher wishes to thank these photographers and organizations for their kind permission to reproduce the following photographs in this book:

7 above Paul Ryan International Interiors; 7 below The Interior Archive / Peter Woloszynski; 8 Inside / Jacques Dirand / design by Rigot; 9 left Marie Claire Maison / Gilles de Chabaneix / Catherine Ardouin; 9 right Robert Harding Picture Library / Adam Woolfitt; 42 below Paul Ryan / International Interiors / Myra Frost; 43 above The Interior Archive / Christopher Simon Sykes; 43 below Paul Ryan / International Interiors / designer Lyn le Grice; 82 above Marie Claire Maison / Marie Pierre Morel / Catherine Ardouin; 82 below Mark Fiennes; 83 above Christian Sarramon; 83 below Marie Claire Maison / Nicolas Tosni / Catherine Ardouin; 114 above Ianthe Ruthven; 114 below Paul Ryan / International Interiors / designer Lyn le Grice; 115 The World of Interiors / Henry Bourne; 138 above Ianthe Ruthven; 138 below The Interior Archive / Jacques Dirand; 139 The Interior Archive / Laura Resen; 162 Inside / Jacques Dirand / design by Rigot; 163 above Ianthe Ruthven; 163 below Jacques Primois.

Special photography was by Debbie Patterson and studio photography by Nicki Dowey. The paint roller illustrations are by Clive Goodyer.